D

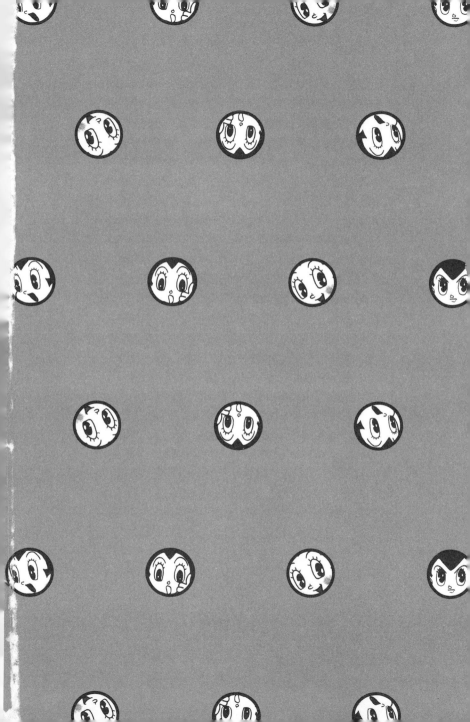

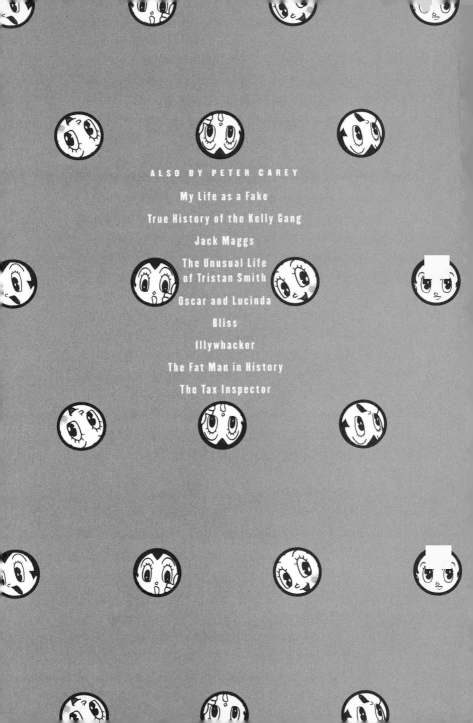

WRONG ABOUT

JAPAN

VOODOO

WRONG ABOUT

ALFRED A. KNOPF, NEW YORK, 2005

JAPAN

PETER CAREY

A FATHER'S JOURNEY WITH HIS SON

THIS IS A BORZOI BOOK PUBLISHED BY ALFRED A. KNOPF

Copyright © 2004 by Peter Carey

All rights reserved under International and Pan-American Copyright Conventions.
Published in the United States by Alfred A. Knopf, a division of Random House, Inc., New York,
and distributed by Random House, Inc., New York.

www.aaknopf.com

Originally published in Australia by Random House Australia, Sydney, in 2004.

Knopf, Borzoi Books, and the colophon are registered trademarks of Random House, Inc.

Permission to reprint previously published material may be found following the illustrations list.

Library of Congress Cataloging-in-Publication Data
Carey, Peter [date]
Wrong about Japan : a father's journey with his son
Peter Carey.—1st ed.
p. cm.
isbn 1-4000-4311-5
1.   Japan—Description and travel.
2.   Carey, Peter, 1943—Travel—Japan.
3.   Fathers and sons—United States.
4.   Fathers and sons—Japan.
5.   Americans—Japan.   I.   Title.
ds812.c27 2005

915.204'5—dc22   2004048425
Manufactured in the United States of America
First American Edition

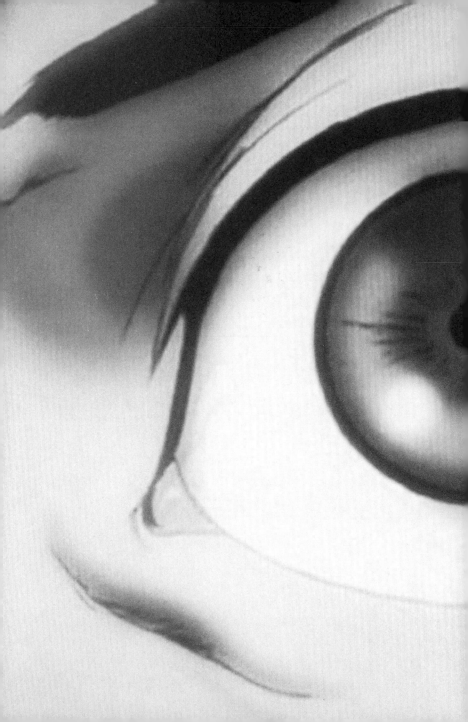

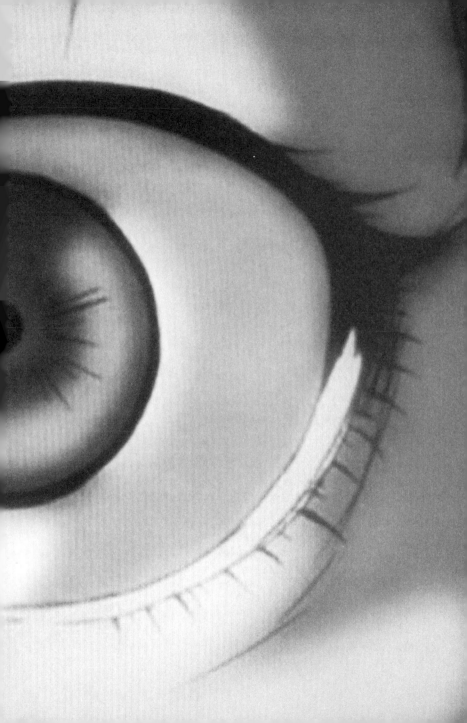

FOR BOTH MY SONS, WITH ALL MY LOVE

WRONG ABOUT JAPAN

1.

I was at the video shop with my twelve-year-old son when he rented *Kikujiro*, a tough-guy/little-boy Japanese film whose charming, twitching hoodlum is played by an actor named Beat Takeshi. How could I have known where this would lead?

Over the next few weeks Charley rented *Kiku-jiro* a number of times, and although I was with him when he did so I had no idea how powerfully he'd been affected, not until he said, quietly, en passant, "When I grow up I'm going to live in Tokyo."

Charley is a shy boy, and later I wondered if he had glimpsed a country where his own character might be seen as admirable. Whether this was true or not, his silent passion for Japan soon broadened, inflamed not only by *Kikujiro* but a whole range of other stimuli. I don't mean that he lay in bed at night reading Tanizaki or Bashō. That would finally be my fate. He was twelve years old. It was the year before Iraq, before he discovered punk rock, NoFX, and Anti-Flag. He and his friends skateboarded. They had Xboxes and GameCubes and PlayStation 2s, and although he read for half an hour a night, he set the timer for exactly thirty minutes and closed the book the instant that it rang. What he then picked up were English translations of Japanese comic books.

These came from stores inhabited by pimply youths sporting green hair and staples in their heads. Forbidden Planet is on lower Broadway, walking distance from our house, and I would accompany him there on Saturday mornings.

Although I knew that Japanese comics were

called *manga*, I would have said that a comic was a comic no matter what you named it. At Forbidden Planet I slowly began to understand that I was wrong. The first and most obvious difference in Japanese comics is the broadness of subject matter, from saccharine stories featuring little big-eyed girls to the dense and serious works of Osamu Tezuka, although this is not something one discovers in a single Saturday morning. What was immediately obvious was the startlingly graphic nature of manga which, in its clarity of line and dramatic blocky forms, echoed the Japanese wood-block prints of the nineteenth century.

Charley and I were soon drifting uptown where, around Grand Central, we found places where the entire English language had been vaporised. Here, in stores catering to Japanese exiles, the graphic nature of manga was more dramatically apparent. Gone were the wordier English translations. Instead, we saw bold hieroglyphics stamped with two or three characters that could be read, although not by us, as unthinkingly as a traffic light.

Charley soon became interested in a comic-book series called Akira—although a comic book is a skinny little thing, whereas a manga has an altogether different heft. Akira would finally run to six volumes with one-inch spines, and I remember how we walked for mile after weary mile in search of a store where the punk-faced slackers might have finally unpacked what we both knew was in their basement: freshly delivered cartons of Akira #6.

Sometimes I was the censor but more often was delighted by artists I never would have discovered if not for my preternaturally tall, crew-cut son. While I never read Akira as attentively as he did, I looked closely enough to understand that it dealt with motorcycle gangs in Neo-Tokyo many years after an atomic devastation. Akira was the name of an immense, malevolent apocalyptic device or person—both, actually—that still lay dormant at the centre of the city. On Akira's graphic pages I found images so artful that I could imagine hanging them on my wall.

Akira, born as manga, had also been made into an animated film which, being Japanese, is not called a cartoon but an anime. It is easy to see why this form should deserve its own label, although less easy to explain why the name is French. Certainly it differs from American animation, which has usually been—with some spectacular exceptions—a dumbed-down form. In America, cartoons are thought to be for kids. In Japan, anime is as much respected as live-action films, and not at all limited to a specific age group. The first anime I saw was based on Akira, and I was immediately struck by the artistry of the frames, their combination of realism, exaggeration, something ineffably and inarguably "Japanese." Once I got hold of a subtitled version and was therefore able to escape the cute Hollywood dubbing, I was at home in a strange, intriguing land. I was as hooked as Charley. I wanted more.

Of course some anime are original, some are shallow, and many are downright silly, but even the really silly ones soon began to seem like artifacts worthy of cultural investigation. For instance, a Japanese clog is called a *geta* and it usually sports two of those devices, which I can only call a "heel"—one at the place its name would lead you to expect, the other at the toe. Why then was that warrior in the anime wearing a clog with just one crazy little stilt, neither at the heel or toe, but at the balance point of the clog? This must mean *something*, even in a silly doodle. I found a reference to the strange clog in Bashō. It didn't solve the mystery, but I began to develop the first of my many misunderstandings, imagining that Bashō's ascetic rural Buddhists wore these clogs because it made walking more difficult. So as my son read manga and glued himself to anime, I began to wonder if we might enter the mansion of Japanese culture through its garish, brightly lit back door.

Later I solved the "heel" puzzle when we talked to a venerable clog maker in Tokyo. "Ah," he said, "you mean a 'one tooth.' " He then explained that a "one tooth" was easier and safer to use in uneven mountain terrain; it was easier, not harder, to walk on.

In any case, I began encouraging Charley to puzzle at the information hidden within manga and anime, and particularly to wonder about what all those foreign characters were doing there. I already knew that the Japanese word *gaijin*, politely translated as "foreigner," literally meant "barbarian." So what did those plentiful foreign characters sound like to a Japanese ear? What sort of accents might these barbarians have? What might their voices signify?

Each night Charley had his thirty minutes of reading literature, but when the timer rang he instantly put down *To Kill a Mockingbird* and picked up Akira. By the time he was into Akira #6, I was reading William Heine's *With Perry to Japan*, Commodore Perry being, of course, the most famous gaijin of them all, the American who "opened up" Japan to trade in 1854.

I interrupted my son's readings to show him the illustrations in my book: nineteenth-century Japanese woodcuts of Perry's big-nosed foreign face. I did not tell him that this nose, in Japanese, meant the gaijin had a very large penis. My point was that these illustrations—given their line, their exaggeration—would have been right at home in a manga. In other words, the high and the low, the historic and the modern, were built on the banks of the same river. As we continued to find these connections, it was only natural that we were soon chatting about the impact of foreigners on Japan, from Perry to MacArthur, not excluding Hiroshima and Nagasaki.

Charley brought home the famous manga about Hiroshima, *Barefoot Gen*. Not to be outdone, I unearthed Studio Ghibli's masterly anime about the firebombing of Tokyo, *Grave of the Fireflies*. If this was pop culture, it was also art and history, and our conversations took an interesting swerve. Coming back from Brooklyn after school one day, my son wondered if I thought the A-bombs would have been dropped had Commodore Perry just stayed at home.

Who knows? Maybe not.

In that case, Charley concluded, there would be no Godzilla.

He wasn't being heartless or trivial. Godzilla had always been a self-conscious Japanese response to the horror of Hiroshima. The monster *was* the bomb.

The kid who would never talk in class was now brimming with new ideas he wasn't shy to discuss. I was excited by him and for him; and for myself too, because I'd already visited Japan twice and now realised I had a perfect pedagogic rationale for indulging my interests further.

"Would you like to go to Japan?" I asked.

"If you like," he said, so dry I couldn't believe it.

"I thought you'd be excited."

His lips flickered and he lowered his eyes. "Not if I have to see the Real Japan."

This alluded to a story I thought he had long forgotten, about an earlier trip I made to Tokyo with my friend Fremantle Jack. While neither of us had been to Japan before, if one of us was going to drive, it definitely should not have been Fremantle Jack, a fine poet but the jitteriest Buddhist I ever met.

As for me, I could recognise only a handful of Japanese characters, and my sense of direction was terrible. I should never have been the navigator. But as we approached the city, I was the one who shouted the directions and Jack who jerked the wheel in response, and that was how—miraculously—we found ourselves on the road to Ginza. I was elated by this serendipity but Fremantle Jack was tugging at his earlobe, not a good sign if you knew him well.

"What's the matter, mate?"

"What's the matter?" he cried. "Are you bloody blind? Look at it!"

The Ikebukurosen, or #5 expressway, was a

concrete ribbon winding—very beautifully, I thought—above the flat roofs of Tokyo which was like nothing I had ever seen: low and chalky white and almost treeless, distinguished by water towers on every building. Even before I got down into the little lanes of Shinjuku, before I walked amongst the perfect Japanese Elvises in Harajuku, before I met Hisao-the-left-handed, who made the most extraordinary chisels on the planet, it was here, on the Ikebukurosen, that I decided to write a science-fiction screenplay, just so we could shoot it in Tokyo.

"It's so *American*," said Jack. "I didn't come all this way for *this*."

"Well, what do you want?"

"I want to see the Real Japan."

I knew what he meant, of course—temples, tea ceremony, Kabuki—but I teased him for it and was doubtless a very irritating companion for the next two weeks.

"No Real Japan," said Charley. "You've got to promise. No temples. No museums."

"What would we do?"

"We could buy cool manga."

"There'll be no English translations."

"I don't care. I'd eat raw fish."

"What else?"

"And slimy things. I'd eat everything."

"What if we interviewed some anime directors?" I asked, trying to figure out how to pay the airfares.

"Could we talk to Tomino?"

"Who's he?"

"Only the director of *Mobile Suit Gundam.*"

"We could talk to people about what all the weird stuff really means."

"Could we meet the guy who did *Godzilla?*"

"Maybe, I don't know."

As the weeks passed, the fantasy hardened into a plan and Charley spent a lot of time eating raw fish and revising the lists of anime directors and manga artists he required me to interview.

"Maybe," I suggested, "you can ask them questions, too."

"Maybe," he said doubtfully. "Can I have an ice cream?"

I was not without contacts in Japan. I wrote first to Paul Hulbert, who was then working for my Tokyo agents. Given their distinguished list of literary authors, I expected he would have little knowledge of cartoons and comic books, so I told him what *Mobile Suit Gundam* was and why I was interested in such a lowly subject.

"Perhaps," he replied, "I should explain a little about myself." Yes, he was a literary agent, of course, but he had previously worked at Kodansha, a large

Japanese publishing house that produced many best-selling manga, including most of the Mobile Suit Gundam series. "During my time there, I worked with manga and anime creators, and in my final year was involved in the production of an eight-hundred-twenty-five-page authorized encyclopedia of the Gundam saga called *Gundam Officials*."

So I began to understand that the fringe cult in New York City was a huge business in Japan, where 1.9 billion manga were sold in 1995—a staggering forty percent of all magazine sales. Everybody in Japan read manga, except those just born or about to die.

Paul said he would certainly arrange an interview with Mr. Tomino, the originator of the Gundam series.

"Could I have my photograph taken with him?" Charley asked.

"Sure."

He bought a map of Tokyo and marked "weird" things with purple stars and "cool" things with silver circles.

His teachers were impressed, and hoped he might give a talk on his return. However, while this new obsession seemed to have briefly transformed him into someone almost garrulous, he had not really changed his character, so when we finally took

off from JFK on the first day of his summer vaca-
tion, there were important words he had not yet
spoken. Only as we landed in Narita did he confess
that he'd made a Japanese friend on the Internet and
this friend would soon come to visit us at the hotel.

"How can he find our hotel?"

"Dad! It's only on the itinerary. I attached it as
a Windows document."

Getting more information was like drawing
teeth. The friend's name was Takashi. He apparently
had no other name. He wanted to practise his English. Yes, he was interested in anime, was that all
right?

"How old is Takashi?"

"Obviously, he's a kid."

"Is he a teenager?"

"A kid. That's all I know."

I would watch this damn Takashi like a hawk. If
he showed the slightest hint of creepiness, he was
gone.

Arriving by train in Tokyo, I lost the Japanese-
language map specifically drawn to get us from the
station to our hotel.

"Don't worry," I said. "It'll be fine."

Later Charley said, "You didn't think it would
be fine at all. You did that thing with your hand like
when you're really stressed out."

"What thing?"

"*That* thing. You know."

Naturally the taxi driver had no English, and yet when he saw our crumpled English map, he didn't sneer like a Manhattan cabbie; he *studied* it, once at the start of the journey and then three more times en route. We were on our way to a *ryokan,* a traditional inn with tatami floors, beds that were rolled away each morning, and a little *tokonoma,* the alcove in which the artful Japanese will display a single precious object. One might assume Tokyo was full of these hotels, but this one, which was also moderately priced, had been very hard to track down, and now seemed impossible to find. The best our driver could do was deposit us at the wrong end of a one-way lane and point with his Mickey Mouse white gloves.

Looking down the lane, I could see mostly parked bicycles and garbage cans, a foreign country where I could not read or speak the simplest phrase. Understanding my hesitation, the driver personally escorted us, running ahead and waving for us to follow, the idling engine of his unlocked cab inviting auto theft.

Touched by his kindness and his poor-man's shoes, I shook his gloved hand.

He, in turn, shook hands with Charley.

"Good-bye," he said. He bowed, then jogged back to his taxi.

The inn is located in the Asakusa district, which

was bombed to dust in World War II. In the nineteenth century when Tokyo was named Edo, Asakusa was a stop on the route from the city to Yoshiwara, the so-called pleasure quarters celebrated in Kabuki and wood-block prints. Soon Asakusa became a pleasure quarter of its own, offering prostitution, Kabuki, and such peculiarly risqué entertainments as female sword fighting. In the streets of Asakusa we recognised the big temple bell from *Kikujiro*, and saw our first transvestite, questionable geisha, pachinko parlour, strip joint, our first drunks sleeping in cardboard boxes. Inside the ryokan was another world entirely—old Japan, kimonos, fish and rice for breakfast.

"Ask if there's a message," Charley said.

"From who?"

"Takashi."

But we were already being escorted to a phone box which turned out to be an elevator, and while we ascended mechanically, the kimonoed maid tore up the stairs, spiralling around us so she might meet us when the lift doors opened on the floor above.

"Watch head," she said, a little out of breath.

The low-ceilinged corridor presented many reasons to "watch head," as we turned left, then right, past the communal bath and into our room which, if spacious in comparison with the lift, was very small indeed. A single bed had been made up on the floor.

"Ah," said the maid, seeing my unhappy face. "So sorry. We thought one person only."

I had sent so many faxes asking for a big room that I am almost certain—and of course I may be wrong—that this was as large a room as two people were going to be allowed. Any bigger and they would've squeezed in three mattresses. Back in the days of travelling salesmen, this is how hotels accommodated them, and you see the economic sense of it. Now that there are no travelling salesmen the hotel stages cultural performances, traditional songs, little plays, big parties, fifty empty beer bottles after breakfast!

"One more mattress, yes?"

"Yes. Where do we put our suitcases?"

"Ah, so sorry. Japanese room."

Yes, that's exactly what the faxes had demanded: a Japanese room, tatami, very minimal. We'd seen it in the movies. Now we resolved to keep it neat, except there was nowhere to hide the luggage, never mind. I never saw a suitcase in the movies.

We had no sooner begun to drink our green tea, sitting cross-legged at a little table that would be pushed to one side at night, than Charley asked me to call Takashi—the first salvo in what would become a constant battle to have me talk instead of him.

"You call," I said. "He's your friend."

"Dad, I have to go to the toilet."

As he closed the door behind him, I resolved that I would not give in this time. He would have to talk himself.

"Come!" he called from the bathroom. "Come now. Quick!"

Whatever he had seen in the bathroom, I knew immediately, was very strange. He'd already seen weird Japanese stuff on the way here—the white-gloved taxi driver, the extraordinary neon-lit shop of pink and orange and blue flowers, a newsstand filled with countless manga with spines two inches thick—but the strangeness he was now negotiating was of a different magnitude.

"Everybody with a taste for traditional architecture," Junichiro Tanizaki wrote in 1933, "must agree that the Japanese toilet is perfection." He then lamented the cost of traditional construction and described his own compromise between cost and custom. "I at least avoided tiles, and had the floor done in camphour wood. To that extent I tried to create a Japanese atmosphere, but was frustrated, finally, by the toilet fixtures themselves. As everyone knows, toilet fixtures are made of pure white porcelain and have handles of sparkling metal. Were I

able to have things my own way, I would much prefer fixtures—both men's and women's—made of
wood. Wood finished in glistening black lacquer is
the very best; but even unfinished wood, as it dark-
ens and the grain grows more subtle with the years,
acquires an inexplicable power to calm and soothe.
The ultimate, of course, is a wooden 'morning glory'
urinal filled with boughs of cedar; this is a delight to
look at and makes not the slightest sound."

"Dad, come *now*! Look!"

God knows what Tanizaki would have thought,
but I was certainly as startled as my son, for the toilet
in our traditional hotel looked like a contraption
designed for a science-fiction comedy. Its arrays of
yellow, red, and blue buttons beside the seat might, as
one could guess, lower or raise the device, convert
the toilet to a bidet or—surely this must have been
my misunderstanding—a shower. However, it was
not immediately clear how one would flush it. Finally
I pushed the blue button and the toilet indeed
flushed, but then water started gushing from a faucet
into a triangular basin in a corner of the room.

We burst out laughing.

It was at just this moment, before we had time
to discover that the seat was electrically heated, that
the telephone rang.

"Please come," a woman said.

"Who is this?"

"Front desk. You come now, please."

"That will be Takashi," said my son, slipping into his shoes in the vestibule.

"Is there a problem?" I asked the woman on the phone.

"Yes. Please come now."

Charley was convinced it was Takashi, though I was equally certain there was a problem with my MasterCard. We bickered amiably while proceeding down the narrow stairs. In the tiled reception, the two young women who'd welcomed us so warmly were still smiling, though differently now, with a sort of grimace of embarrassment. Credit card, I thought, credit card for sure!

The elder, she was no more than thirty, did not speak. Instead she made a gesture that foreigners are taught is more polite than pointing: not one finger, but all five digits together like a slap. Looking in the direction this indicated, I saw, by the wide doorway to the lane, in front of the antique calligraphic banner and beside the picturesque sake barrels, the most singular boy. It was not just his hair, or his eyes, or his clothes that distinguished him. There was a certain quality of *light* he seemed to have brought in with him, one quite distinct from the deep shadows and glowing gold tones of the ryokan, something more like that clean white, almost hallucinogenic illumination in a Tokyo department store. He literally *shone.*

I looked at Charley. How happy he seemed.

This must be Takashi, I did not doubt it.

In Tokyo's Harajuku district one can see those perfect Japanese Michael Jacksons, no hair out of place, and punk rockers whose punkness is detailed so fastidiously that they achieve a polished hyper-reality. Takashi had something of this quality. He had black hair that stood up not so much in spikes but in dramatic triangular sections. His eyes were large and round, glistening with an emotion that, while seemingly transparent, was totally alien to me. He wore a high-necked Cambridge blue jacket with what might have once been called a Mao collar, and which glistened with gold buttons. His trousers were jet black, his boots knee high. No one could doubt his pride, or his sense of dignity.

"Charley-san?" he asked, and bowed.

My son also bowed.

The women in kimonos looked straight ahead as if none of this was happening.

"Perhaps we can take tea," I suggested.

I had earlier noted a little salon just beside reception. Here, I assumed, such meetings might be held, but there was something about Takashi that— so sorry—made this salon temporarily unavailable. The three of us were ushered back up to our room, and tea was brought to us in this fine and private place.

When the maid left us, Takashi said, "You have cable here, Charley-san?"

They turned together to evaluate the very small television set beside our two suitcases.

"I guess so," Charley said. "We just got here."

I invited Takashi to inspect the television. "Very nice," he said, even though there were only three channels and we were reduced to watching a demonstration of a device sucking wax from a man's ear. There was a close-up of brown material in a bowl.

"Very clever," said Takashi. "You have a very nice hotel. Old style."

"Difficult to keep neat," I said. "We have nowhere to put the suitcases."

"Yes," he said. "Everyone owns many things. In the old days, the rich families, they would have a storehouse for their stuffu."

"Stuffu?"

"Stuffu," he said again, then turned to Charley. "You know, stuffu."

"Stuff, Dad," Charley said. "Worldly goods."

"The merchants got so rich, but it was against the law for them to be higher than the samurai. Still, they have lots of stuffu. Dangerous for them to show off, I think. Cut their head off if they get too high. So nice they build a simple house, looks simple, but very expensive to make. And they show just one expensive thing at a time, here in the tokonoma."

This was the only time I heard this intriguing suggestion, that the origins of the tokonoma lay in the old sumptuary laws.

"These days everyone has stuffu. I show you."

And he produced from deep inside his coat a little photographic book called *Tokyo: A Certain Style,* whose hundreds of untidy teenage rooms turned out to be the apartments of Tokyo designers, musicians, software inventors, Swatch collectors, publicists, editors, not one of them displaying anything like what you would call a Japanese aesthetic. They looked more like Charley's bedroom in Manhattan and my son fell hungrily upon the thick square volume, identifying everything, item by item, brand name by brand name—Xbox, GameCube, Game Boy—stuffu.

"Dad," he said, "this is so cool. There are things here I never saw before."

"Very Japanese," said Takashi. "This is what I said I would show you and your father, Charley-san. This week you will see the real Japan. You saw pictures of temples?" he asked me.

"One or two," I admitted.

"Yes, rocks, gravel, nice Japanese room, so simple. Houses with rough timber?"

"Yes," I said. "Very beautiful."

"Real Japanese people not like that." Takashi smiled.

I made my polite open-palm gesture toward the atomic toilet. "I understand," I said. "More modern."

Takashi got up and peered into the bathroom. "No, this is American."

"But we don't have these toilets in the United States."

"Perhaps you are from Australia? Soon you will go to Macy's in New York. You will see. In any case, I will show you these toilets here, in Akihabara Electric Town. But now you are tired. We can meet at Akihabara."

"Where is that?"

"Everyone will know it. Akihabara on the JR line. At the station go to exit three." He then produced a small gift-wrapped box and handed it to Charley. "Something you use in Tokyo," he said. "You find me anywhere."

We all stood, bowing in the little room. He stepped off the tatami and somehow managed to slip into his tall boots as easily as if they were a pair of slippers. Only when he'd left did we discover what his gift was: a wafer-thin iridescent orange object which, when opened, revealed itself to be a phone with a skittishly active little screen.

My first thought was that this was far too expensive, but Takashi's carefully handwritten note explained he was simply lending it to us for our visit.

"You see this, Dad?" Charley was holding up a little string of luminous beads attached to the bottom of the phone. "You know what this is for?"

"No."

"It stops cancer."

"Charley!"

"Dad, you don't know. It deflects the microwaves from the phone."

"Oh, I see. What else does it do?"

"Sends text."

"In Japanese?"

"In English. If you want to send in Japanese it's harder."

"How do you know this?"

But he was busy already with his thumbs.

"Okay, that's enough. We're going out to eat."

"Can I take the cell?"

"No."

"Please."

"No, you'll fiddle all through dinner."

"Can I leave it in the tokonoma?"

"Yes. Yes, yes. Now let's go."

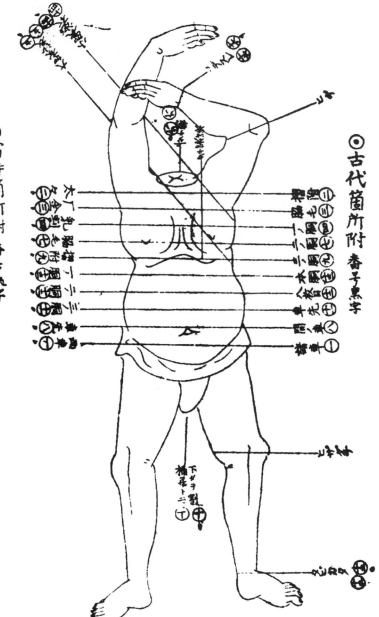

2.

On the Internet, I found this blurb for the anime *Blood: The Last Vampire*: "On an American military base in Japan, a new kind of vampire emerges: Ter-opterids, monstrous shape-shifting creatures that can only be killed by special swords. A mysterious girl named Saya is the last 'original,' the only person capable of dealing with the menace. Posing as a student at the base's school, Saya races to hunt down the beasts before they turn an ordinary Halloween bash into a bloody massacre. Production IG, known for their pioneering digital effects, describes *Blood: The Last Vampire* as a full digital animation movie, which means that even though many sequences were animated using pencil and paper, the artwork was digitally scanned. Inking and coloring were completed by computer, as were several other special effects. Hiroyuki Kitakubo was chosen to direct the project because of his digital experience."

I had never been the tiniest bit interested in vampires, nor did I have any taste for blood seeping, squirting, or splashing, not even the high-culture blood of Medea's children. Yet Kitakubo's *Blood: The Last Vampire* held an eerie attraction for me. This was partly to do with its unusual style, the result of juxtaposing a densely realistic world with graphically animated characters; but what really made my heart beat faster was a story packed full of coded Japanese attitudes toward controlling foreigners. Here we have an American base on Japanese soil, and most importantly, that "special sword" which Saya wields so passionately. Aware that Westerners were commonly thought incapable of understanding the Japanese sword, I asked my Japanese translator's assistant, Jeremy Hedley, if he could contact Kitakubo, and arrange a meeting.

Jerry wrote back: "Just a quick note to see if you want to take this any further. Got in touch with the studio that made *Blood: The Last Vampire* (Production IG) to see whether it's possible to meet Kitakubo, the director. Spoke with a PR rep there and received confirmation that the triumph of business over art and kindness is now complete: they want to know what's in it for them. . . ."

Well, nothing—except that I could perhaps tell the story of the film.

When we first see her, Saya is a very solemn young girl, perhaps sixteen years old, sitting all alone in a subway car. The visual effect of this scene is startling, the surroundings rendered in realistic digital detail, the girl drawn loosely, seemingly illuminated by multiple light sources—overhead fluorescents, luminescent bulbs in the subway tunnel which strobe across her. Her clothes are black, her skin white, lips red, and there is a steely, withdrawn yet hostile aspect to her. She has stiffened up the sinews, disguised fair nature with hard-favoured rage. She is obviously a warrior.

At the far end of the same car is a sleeping man, or perhaps (and this remains tantalisingly unclear) an alien life form, a Teropterid, who has assumed the body of a man. Now Saya rises, sword drawn. As she rushes down the carriage I think of *The Seven Samurai*, but also of the novelist Yukio Mishima, who used his sword to commit ritual suicide by disembowelment. I recall also the camera panning across the devastation of firebombed Tokyo in the opening scenes of the anime *Grave of the Fireflies*. An officer standing in the middle distance cries "Long live the Emperor!" before plunging his sword into his belly, although the camera gives him no more attention than any other landmark of a country apparently dying in agony. Such is the power of the Japanese sword to fascinate me, creep me out. How not to be repulsed by the blood splattering across the windows of the subway car?

At Asakusa Station, a five-minute walk from our hotel, Saya meets with her American handlers who might be military or CIA. She tells them her sword is not sharp enough. We see them not listening, not understanding. It is so clear, even to me, that these Americans are ignorant about swords. In desperation, Saya then steals a sword that shows every sign of being a great Japanese antique, but she is not a connoisseur and not until the sword breaks in battle with the Teropterids does it reveal itself a counterfeit. The sword Saya wanted, Charley and I would soon discover, could have been forged only in a long and complicated process in which molten steel had been divided and refolded hundreds of times. Hard steel would then be wrapped around a soft steel core. Finally, its edge would be hard and sharp enough—believe me, I've seen the illustrations—to cleave a man from left shoulder to right hip. A true Japanese sword has a flexible inner core and would not have betrayed Saya in battle.

All this, and many other things, I wished to discuss with Mr. Kitakubo. My son desired the meeting just as badly, but for a different reason: he wanted to be photographed next to an anime hero. How cool would that be? Kitakubo would become a trophy hanging on a Manhattan bedroom wall.

That first night in Tokyo, this carefully orchestrated plan was threatened when a fax arrived from Jerry. Like me, Jerry is Australian and fifteen years in Tokyo have left him blessedly profane. "This PR at Production IG is being a real dickhead. Earlier he told me that Kitakubo would determine the location for your meeting. Now we're being told that, no, *we* must do that. Suggested a cheesy American-style 'family restaurant' but can't confirm the damned thing until the PR hears back from Kitakubo and then makes contact to say this location is okay. Very good news however, the sword maker will see us tomorrow morning. Will call you early to confirm where we shall meet."

As the train carrying Saya and the corpse of her victim arrives at the station, an announcer declares it Asakusa, the last stop. This, as it happened, was where we agreed to meet Jerry and his wife, Etsuko.

When, the night before, Charley and I stepped out into the warm blue Asakusa night, he asked where we were going.

"We'll find something nice to eat," I said.

"Have you got a map?"

"No."

"Then you don't know where we are?"

We wandered blindly along lanes so narrow that the driver of a Toyota had to move parked bicycles in order to pass through. Meanwhile, I realised I couldn't tell the difference between a restaurant and a house of ill repute. Nor did I know that we were staying in the heart of Japanese pop culture, of Kabuki, *kodan*, *manzai*, *rakugo*, *kamishibai*, all the hundred forms of Japanese storytelling, several of which were directly connected to the birth of manga and anime.

Entering the wide street we would soon name "Drunk Street," we walked between the pachinko and off-track betting parlours and discovered a large covered arcade with many restaurants. Here we stood, staring at the plastic food in the window. Not a word of English in sight.

"I don't think this is a good area, Dad."

I did not doubt him, but we were hungry. "It's fine," I said.

"This is not a good area."

Heedless, I led him inside a restaurant. Immediately we were sent back to the window to study the plastic food. Then we were joined by a raffish gentleman, roughly sixty years old, with grey slicked-back hair, baggy light-coloured trousers, a pair of very loud yellow braces, and a tie of equal volume. His face had a smooth, rather pampered quality.

"Perhaps you like the soup," he said, "or you might have the shrimp, see, very nice." He smiled, then used the five-fingered point. "Or you can have this together with the shrimp. Eat both together."

"Okay," said Charley.

"Also there is the buckwheat noodle."

"I'll just have the noodles," said Charley.

"Or perhaps you like the rice. There is also sashimi, but not cooked. Very Japanese. What you like?"

"The noodles, thank you."

Our benefactor then arranged a superior table, and instructed the waiter in detail, a beer for me and a cola for Charley.

"See," I told my son, "these are very nice people. This is a good place." At the same time I was wondering if he was noticing the girls in geisha costumes as they tripped down the front stairs and set off into the night, singing their charming little singsong good nights like canaries in a cage. Were they really geishas? Of course not.

"Ah, you use chopsticks very well," said our protector as he reappeared.

Charley, who has never liked being the object of scrutiny, said nothing.

"Yes," our protector said at last, "that is one very good way to eat this dish." He paused. "Also another way. You can put the shrimp in with the soup if you like."

Charley nodded, but he hadn't asked for the shrimp and he was not about to eat it now.

"Ah yes," our guide said politely, "the way you are doing it—this is a very good way, too."

When he had gone, Charley leaned forward.

"Dad, you know where we are?"

"Where?"

He rolled his eyes.

"What?"

"Nothing, Dad. Not now."

Only when we stood in the arcade, looking out through the summer rain at the desolation of Drunk

Street, did my son tell me what was on his mind. "Did you look behind you?"

"What was behind me?"

"Did you see the chef? He was like a sumo wrestler. He was scary. He had bright orange hair. And the guys around him, they were really scary too."

"I didn't notice."

"Did you see the girls coming down the stairs?"

"Of course. They were geisha."

My twelve-year-old rolled his eyes. "Dad, this is what they call an Entertainment Area."

Irony about a subject he couldn't possibly comprehend? "In any case," I said hurriedly, "the old man was very nice to you. He reminded me of my own father."

"That would be funny."

"Why?"

"Because he was a yakuza."

"You think he's a gangster because he has a loud tie?"

"And those suspenders."

Frankly, I thought Charley had seen too many subtitled gangster movies, but when, the next day, we met up with Jerry and Etsuko, they thought he was probably correct.

Together we finally left Asakusa, heading north

on a train toward the sword maker. From our carriage we had a view of Tokyo that somehow didn't seem to count, the area between the centre and the airport. For all I had mocked Fremantle Jack, I was just as guilty: I had noticed these rather boring suburban vistas coming in from Narita, but the Real Japan, I felt, lay elsewhere. Even now, as we sped past concrete, plastic pipes nailed, stapled, screwed, tied onto stucco, steel, aluminium, a cacophony of pale blue roof, rusty steel, glazed faux slate, heavy electric posts with finned drummed transformers, even now as we rattled beside convex insulators, crossbars holding pale grey boxes entwined by heavy black cable from which, like nerves from ganglia, thinner black cables issued, even as we passed kitchen windows with detergent bottles displayed as in a tokonoma, I waited to arrive somewhere where a sword maker might really live.

This landscape was of no interest to my son; his thumbs were already busy on his text messenger, as fast as the teenagers on the other side of the car.

"Are you writing to Takashi?"

"Yes."

"Well, we're at the station now."

But as we descended the stairs, walked across the rails, and entered the deserted suburban streets, he was still in nimble conversation, bringing up the rear. Jerry and I formed the centre, Etsuko walking a little ahead of us, consulting directions on a piece of pale blue paper.

Japanese addresses rightly seem complicated to gaijin. Say your friend's address is 1-12-33 Asakusa Chome, Taito-ku. This means your friend lives in Taito Ward, in the district of Asakusa. Within Asakusa you will need to find area number one. If you're well prepared you'll have a map; if not, you ask a local. Then you use the same process to find block 12 and there, sooner or later, you'll find building number 33. Of course it will be nowhere near building 32 or 34. It is more likely to be sandwiched between 20 and 7. Imagine what this did to the minds of the American occupation forces in 1945. No street names. Meaningless numbers. The victors changed many things about Japan, and for many of these—for instance the first democratic government in the nation's history—most Japanese are grateful. But the American plan to render the Japanese addresses "more logical" never had a hope in hell.

"It is not because we are secretive," Takashi told me later. "Westerners think we want to hide from them. No one is hiding. Our way is logical. It is zoom shot, see. Begin wide, then zoom in until you have CU of your building."

"CU?"

"Close-up. Charley will know CU when he goes to film school. You zoom in on where you want to go."

Thus Etsuko set to zoom in on the sword maker, Yoshindo Yoshihara, in Katsushika Ward. She skirted ahead, darting right and left while the rest of us dawdled behind, my son still engaged in thumb-talk: WHERE CAN U GET COOL MOBILE SUIT GUNDAM MODELS, or words to that effect. In the great suburban silence I could hear his clicking, and then the sound of wooden clogs on bitumen. A well-preserved man of perhaps fifty rounded the corner. He wore crisply pressed corduroy trousers and his geta, his clogs, were a gorgeous honeyed yellow.

"Ah," said the man, in answer to Etsuko. "Yoshihara-san!" Then he began walking her to the corner and pointing.

"Turn it off," I hissed.

"In a minute," said Charley.

"Now!"

Etsuko finally matched the numbers on a gate to the address on her piece of paper. I saw a pile of bright long metal rods stacked against the side of an outbuilding, a sign of light industry that appeared out of place in this neighbourhood.

As Charley reluctantly slipped his phone into the leg pocket of his baggy jeans, we crossed a lovely mossy garden through which a small brook ran—not something one might have imagined when staring out the window of the Narita Express.

Yoshihara-san greeted us politely, but as the four of us huddled in his doorway I had the sudden, shocking sense that while the surroundings seemed rather ordinary, we were disturbing a highly distinguished fellow. Even before we were ushered into a parlour and Yoshihara-san asked what we wished to know, I felt out of my depth, like a day-tripper who has somehow found himself in the presence of Picasso.

The room was at once suburban and not. Along one wall stood tall thick books, their spines marked in Japanese characters, and also a warrior's helmet, obviously very old. On an adjacent wall were displayed some tiny model swords in brightly coloured scabbards. Through glass doors I could see a diorama of family life: a baby, a toddler, a larger son, a pretty wife.

What did we want to know? Well, I certainly wasn't about to talk to this man about cartoons. Instead, I recalled what was written in *The Japanese Sword: The Soul of the Samurai*: "Traditionally the forging of a Japanese sword took place in near-religious conditions. The smithy would be purified by a Shinto priest and would have a sacred rice-straw rope (*shimenawa*) with sacred paper (*gohei*) attached as symbols of purity, erected to surround the smithy."

So I asked if making a sword felt like a spiritual business to him.

Yoshihara-san smiled. "You've been reading American books?"

"English," I admitted.

"Perhaps some people have spiritual experiences. They hear voices talking to them. Then they are crazy."

Later Charley said, "He was very energetic. He laughed a lot."

Indeed he did. He also had bright, challenging eyes and an attractive earthiness.

I asked him if he did not sometimes think about the function of the sword as he forged it, that it was made to cut skin and flesh, to take life.

No, Yoshihara-san replied. He never thought about the sword this way. "Never."

I said nothing of the diagram I had seen, one which shows the human body overlaid with a catalogue of different cuts that the sword appraisers of the Edo period used on condemned or recently executed prisoners.

What he concentrated on, Yoshihara-san explained, was how to make the sword.

And why should I doubt him? The making of the Japanese sword is a very exacting business, requiring the steel be folded and refolded on itself until it had formed the most extraordinary molecular bonds, some of which, when the sword is finally polished, will show like clouds, summer lightning, ghosts running parallel to the edge of death.

Yoshihara-san claimed to think only of the sword. But later I read his book *The Craft of the Japanese Sword*, in which he wrote that you cannot make a sword unless you understand its function. By the time I came across this apparent inconsistency, it was too late to ask the author if the "function" of the sword could be anything other than death.

One can guess that the romance of the sword relates to the samurai, men who fought fiercely for their lord's honour as well as their own, who lived each day in a state of preparation for death, so proud that rather than surrender to an enemy, or in atonement for their own failure, or because their lord was dying in battle, would use their swords to disembowel themselves.

Of course, the Japanese sword is no longer used in war. Forbidden to be worn in public, it is instead collected, the subject of connoisseurship, although one cannot help but imagine that its deadly power lends an essential frisson to its icy beauty.

An untested instrument of death must always carry with it a certain tension, and in the case of the Japanese sword this is by no means a modern issue. During the long, peaceful reign of the Tokugawa Shogunate, which began more than four centuries ago, the power of the sword and its esteemed owner was already problematic. The samurai retained the right to cut down anyone of lower rank who offended them, and as they were the upper class in a society which valued nothing more than honour, surely offence was easily found. But there was no war, so what could a warrior do? By the eighteenth century most samurai had never seen a battle.

In *The Taming of the Samurai,* Eiko Ikegami discusses the diary of one Edo-period samurai, Bunzaemon, who had become, in the midst of this long peace, a habitué of the theatre and a student of the formerly aristocratic arts of No and flower arranging. There were many like him. He was an unremarkable man, a conformist who, Ikegami reports, "liked to reenact the older traditions of samurai valour. . . . [He] entered a school of martial arts when he was eighteen. He participated in the sword-testing session, in which samurai tried out new swords during the execution of prisoners sentenced to death, or cut their bodies into smaller pieces afterward. Bunzaemon was excited about cutting into a human body, something he believed every true samurai should experience."

I asked Yoshihara-san what made the sword so important to the Japanese people, so important that its artisans might, in the year 2003, still be declared National Living Treasures. He said he could not explain it to me.

In the two hundred and thirty peaceful years before the arrival of Commodore Perry's "black ships," the samurai entered the bureaucracy of the shogunate, and by the seventeenth century they had become bureaucrats, known by military titles and organised along military lines. Reading of their lives, one sees them slowly metamorphose into an antecedent of today's *sarariman*. Being samurai, of course, Bushido was their code of honour.

In June 2002 *The Way of Bushido* was a best-seller in Tokyo. Japanese businessmen apparently found this book very useful. As with the secret fascination with the sword, this "useful" quality appears difficult to explain to Westerners.

The swords of World War II stay with us not because they were finely made—they were not—but because of how enthusiastically these essentially medieval weapons were wielded by their owners. It was not too many weeks after my visit to Tokyo that I was in Penang talking to a retired schoolteacher who was a boy at the time of the Japanese invasion. He recalled, in chilling detail, the terror of rolling heads, fluttering eyelids, blood spurting to the level of the roofs. I would also suggest that the Japanese themselves understand exactly why the sword might be repulsive.

Yoshihara-san's grandfather Kuni-ie was a legendary sword maker who had forged swords for the emperor himself, a fact that Yoshihara-san modestly never mentioned. When the making of swords was outlawed in 1945, Yoshihara-san's father abandoned the craft forever. However, Kuni-ie continued, and in 1953, when the law once more permitted him practise of the craft, he accepted his grandson as his student. Thus Yoshihara-san, now amongst the most celebrated swordsmiths in the world, became the tenth generation of his family to forge these legendary blades.

I had hoped we would be shown a sword here, just once, but now I understood this could never be. We would not know the etiquette, how to sit, how to hold the scabbard, or the hilt, how to slide the blade out by the back surface only. We were gaijin, capable only of hurting the sword or ourselves. Yes, we probably would notice the *hamon*, those wistful clouds and waves dancing within the molecules of steel, poems written along the edge of death, but to see them in any profound way would take at least three years of constant study, not a one-hour visit on a Monday morning.

In any case, I could see that Charley was bored out of his brain. He sat on the sofa with his hands folded on his lap, his shoulders slumped in early teenage melancholy. It was time to go. Just the same, I asked if we might see where Yoshihara-san worked, and so we crossed the mossy garden again and entered a sturdy, high-roofed structure with a brick floor and two very simple kilns that looked more like rough stone troughs. My son, it was obvious, was waiting for the time to pass. For his father, however, it was a pleasant place to be, so clean and orderly. Along one wall, near the kiln, were hung some thirty different sets of tongs. Remembering that the traditional Japanese carpenters once used something like forty different planes, and had a name for each, I asked if these tongs had names.

He shrugged. His no did not require translation.

"What do you ask your apprentice to pass you then?"

"Apprentice?" He laughed. "I lean across and get it myself."

I asked him about *yaki-ire*, the stage of the process where the smith, working at night, must correctly judge the colour of the heated blade before plunging it into water to harden it. The literature suggests that the colour of the steel ideally matches that of the full moon in February and August, and many of the famous swords of antiquity are dated with these months.

In his own book, Yoshihara and his collaborators write: "Yaki-ire—the process of heating a sword until it is red hot, and then plunging it into a trough of water—is perhaps the most dramatic moment in the swordsmith's day. In the popular imagination, the glowing blade, the darkened smithy, the hissing billow of steam—all these make yaki-ire an almost mystical enterprise, whereby the metal structure of the blade is itself transformed, and a sword is born.

"The practical reality here, as is so often the case, is quite different. Yaki-ire is all in a day's work, and as often as not ends in a ruined blade that must be either reworked or discarded. It is performed at night with the lights out so the smith must be able to see the true colour of the naked blade in order to judge its temperature. . . ."

When I asked Yoshihara about forging swords at night, he once more made me feel hopelessly romantic. He worked in the gloom, he said, not at night. But his book gives a more complete answer: "People live at close quarters here, and sword making can be very noisy work. Yoshindo [Yoshihara] and Shoji [his youngest brother] are currently the only two swordsmiths working within the Tokyo city limits. In deference to their neighbours they restrict their hammering and folding of steel to the hours between nine and five on weekdays."

We had come a long way from comic strips, or so it seemed, for just a moment.

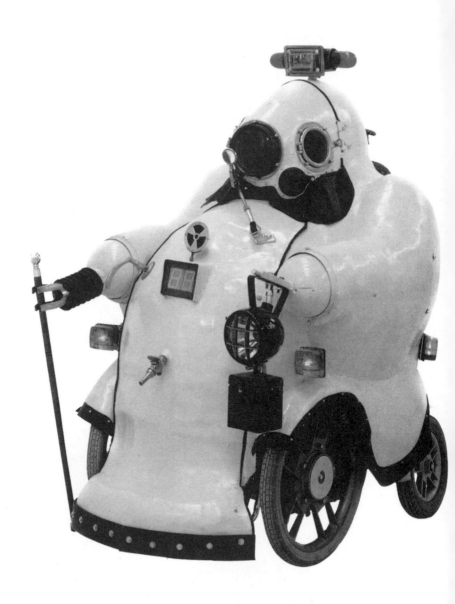

3.

On two occasions in Tokyo, I spoke with Kosei Ono, not only a cartoonist but a highly respected critic of manga and anime, who put all of his considerable erudition at my service. Our final meeting, however, must have alarmed him. In preparing for my meeting with Mr. Yoshihara I had read a number of books about the Japanese sword and had noted that the word *saya* meant "sheath." Saya also happened to be the name of the proud, angry swordswoman in *Blood: The Last Vampire.* My mistake was not in pointing this out to Kosei but allowing a sort of mad excitement to show in my eyes as I did so.

Returning to New York, I found Kosei's letter awaiting me. Typically it contained all sorts of tantalising information, including the fact that the artwork in *Blood: The Last Vampire* was done by the manga artist Katsuya Terada, who was strongly influenced by such American comic-book artists as Mike Mignola, who in turn was influenced by Jack Kirby, the creator of Captain America. Having offered such gifts, Kosei came to a point that must have been worrying him since we said good-bye in Tokyo. He pointed out that so many characters, while pronounced the same way, have quite different meanings. In any case, he continued, "girl's name will never mean 'sheath,' which is too obvious for Japanese people. . . . Well, so much for today. Be careful, half knowledge is sometimes much worse than complete ignorance. Sorry for my terrible English. Regards, Kosei."

Reading his very polite letter occasioned a depressing feeling that stemmed from my shameful ignorance. I'd felt much the same way as we walked away from Yoshihara-san's workshop without having so much as *glimpsed* a sword.

It had been a grey, overcast day in the sword-smith's suburb. Now my inability to even break the skin of this culture became somehow entangled with this melancholy light and also my feelings about my son, who was slouching slowly towards the train station with his head bowed over the cell phone. Naturally it did not occur to me that he was already adapting to a certain Japanese language; that is, he could do thumb-talk in a way that would forever elude his clumsy father.

"Look around you," I said irritably. "See where you are. You're not on Bleecker Street now."

"I *am* looking," he said.

At the screen, he meant.

"Takashi wants to know," he said, "can we go to Sega World?" He held up the iridescent orange instrument. Cut into its seething sci-fi screen was a text message. "He says they have really cool games there."

"We didn't fly for eighteen hours to go to a video arcade."

"Dad, you forget. Sega World is at Akihabara."

"Akihabara?"

"Electric Town—remember? You read about it.

You wanted us to go there. It's in *Little Adventures in Tokyo*."

He was right. According to Rick Kennedy, the author of this handy guidebook: "The place spills over with raw commercial energy and off-the-rails electronic wizardry. It is gaudy and jarring, exhausting and exhilarating. It is the world's most high-powered bazaar, with everything always on sale, from voltmeters and logic analyzers to miniature washing machines for miniature apartments . . . [from] tea-serving robots to solar-powered ice cream makers and pogo sticks with battery-operated digital readout of time-hopped."

"It was your idea," my son said indignantly. "You said it was filled with cool stuff, Dad. We could buy a Japanese toilet and take it home for Mom. Just joking."

"We haven't even seen a sword yet. Wouldn't you like to go to the sword museum first?"

But of course I knew the answer. Throughout my failure of an interview with Mr. Yoshihara, Charley had waited politely just as I myself had once waited as my father sold GM cars to farmers. Now it was my son's turn to enjoy the trip he had been promised.

"Give me some change," he said. "I'll get the tickets for Akihabara. Please . . ."

I gave him a handful of coins, and by the time Jerry, Etsuko, and I caught up with him, Charley was feeding a very alien-looking ticket dispenser as if it were a Vegas slot machine. Now he was alive, engaged. The machine whirred at his command, spitting tickets out into his waiting hand.

"How do you know how to do that?"

"I'm going to live here," he said, "after my band fails."

The Tokyo subway is big and complicated. The lines are owned by different companies, some of whom accept each other's tickets, some of whom don't. Of course I should take Charley to Akihabara—this was his trip after all—but now I saw that he was somehow taking me.

"You are a different species," I told him.

"We mutated," he corrected.

Even on the JR Yamanote Line he showed no interest in what was outside the window. Instead, he studied the map, running his fingers along the dense-coloured lines as if reading a circuit in braille. He led the transfer of subway lines at Asakusa and again at Ueno. At Akihabara he slipped our tickets into a machine marked "Fare Adjustment," and I gave him the two hundred yen he asked for. He then located exit three, where his strange friend was waiting for us.

Takashi bowed to Etsuko, Jerry, and me, but his greeting with Charley was a complicated handshake ending in a shoulder slam.

"Carey-san," he said to me, "we will see toilets."

Hearing this news, Etsuko excused herself. She had a job to go to.

Walking a little ahead, Charley and Takashi presented a clear contrast. Charley, tall and twelve years old, wore rumpled New York street clothes. Takashi was perhaps fifteen but a head shorter. His black Japanese hair, even in its wild dishevelment, was crisp and clean as knife blades. There was not a spot or wrinkle on him. Every detail of his tunic was pristine, pressed, as if just released from a polythene wrap.

"Who the hell is he?" I asked Jerry. "*What* is he?"

As the two boys pushed through the crowds beneath the railway bridge on Chuo Dori, I remembered Charley's joke. *"We mutated."*

"First," Jerry said, "he is a character from anime. All that romantic military stuff, the boots and the coat—I'd say he was out of Mobile Suit Gundam."

Of all the thousands of anime series, this one I actually knew about because it was Charley's favourite. In Mobile Suit Gundam the kids fight endless, politically complex wars from inside giant robots. In fact, Charley and I had an appointment to interview Yoshiyuki Tomino, who originated the series, as I now reminded Jerry.

"Well"—he smiled—"doesn't he look like a Tomino character to you?"

"He does rather."

But Jerry had already moved on. "He is also what is called a visualist. You think Japanese are great conformists. Remember, though, that this was a country which once had strict laws about what you wore, where you lived. God help you if you acted like a samurai when you weren't. Can you imagine what it feels like to wear what you damn well please? You want to be a robot pilot, that's your choice. I was in Mitsukoshi, the department store, and there was this extraordinary transvestite. He had that same crazed sense of detail—an amazing hat, stacked high with fruit like Carmen Miranda's. And he was just standing in the middle of the store with everyone walking around him, pretending he wasn't there. But he was perfect, in every single detail. That's what a visualist does. My friend's neighbour likes to dress up as a traditional carpenter—the flared trousers, the two-toed socks, the whole kit. By day he's an accountant working for a conservative newspaper, and he goes home on the subway looking like a conformist. But then he's not only got the clothes, he's got a bloody carpenter's *truck* and he goes out cruising."

"Where does he go cruising?"

"No place we could take Charley."

"And?"

"He picks up girls. Carpenters have lots of money. Also: go to Harajuku Station and see the kids round there. Elvis, Michael Jackson, Perfect Reproduction Punks. But this is not just a modern thing. Stuff like this was going on in the seventeenth century when it was much more dangerous. In 1600 young men with fuck-you clothes began appearing in the big cities. They were called Kabuki Mono, Kabuki meaning 'crooked' or 'deviant and licentious.' Reading about them, they seem exactly like punks. Some of them wore imported velvet collars, short kimonos, with lead weights in the hems. I guess you could say they were visualists as well."

By now we had come to the bustle of Kuramaebashi Dori, and with the kids walking quickly ahead, I was anxious not to lose them. As we pursued them, I asked Jerry what he could tell about Takashi.

"Not much."

"Well, can you tell his class?"

"Japanese don't really have class-differentiated accents."

"Is he well educated? Educated at all?"

"Perhaps."

"Is he gay, do you think?"

"Who would know?"

By now we were in Akihabara, the true belly of the beast, entering a six-storey maze, every floor and corner of it bursting with that neon light Tanizaki so abhorred. Not for nothing is this Electric Town. White and silver and candy-coloured manufactured surfaces glowed in the dustless, conditioned air. Price tags hung from the ceilings in fluorescent orange and red and green and blue. Actually, they may not have been price tags, but the names of fish or the days of the week. We wandered from floor to floor. Stuffu everywhere—plasma screens, cell phones as thin as credit cards with guerilla war playing on their screens, those crazy science-fiction toilets, fifteen models at least.

But had we come to Japan to look at such mundane appliances? In search of stronger stuff, we entered a labyrinth of lanes, arcades where it was not always clear where one business ended and another began. Like Luke Skywalker and Han Solo looking for spare parts on the planet Xenon, we browsed in dusty little shops selling mammoth radio valves, tiny black items identified only by the number on the box and sometimes by a small yellow stripe like a vein of candy sandwiched in a block of licorice.

There was plenty of noise, but nothing like the barrage that awaited us in Sega World: five floors devoted to terrifying arcade games where kids with guns shoot men like fish in a bucket. This was before Iraq made the doubling of war and fantasy so ominous. But war had been much on my mind before we came to Japan, and I was searching in every cultural artifact for echoes of the atomic bomb, the firebombing of Tokyo, the American occupation, the manner in which a proud and isolated society had waged war, suffered war, emerged from war.

In New York, Charley had broken his NO MUSEUMS rule to visit the Brooklyn Museum of Art for a show called *My Reality: Contemporary Art and the Culture of Japanese Animation.* There we encountered the work of Kenji Yanobe, sculptures created on a carlike scale. According to the catalogue: "Yanobe's playful atomic cars are a cross between robots and Volkswagen Beetles, but deal with the horrific idea of surviving a nuclear holocaust. Bold colors and shiny surfaces display Geiger counters, flashing lights, radiation penetration counters, heating stems, and disposals. Both science fiction and cartoon, the cars encapsulate their drivers and provide for their survival." The cars are cute and funny, but also terrifying and claustrophobic. You cannot look at them without thinking of both the poisoning of the earth and the isolation of the individual in urban postindustrial society.

To my mind, there a distinct parallel between Yanobe's work and the Mobile Suit Gundam anime that, thanks to Charley, I was already familiar with. Originally televised in 1979, this phenomenon features giant robots, popularly known as Mobile Suits, "piloted" by young soldiers in the throes of an intergalactic war. Before leaving New York I had already begun a correspondence with Yoshiyuki Tomino, Gundam's creator, with whom I brashly shared many of my opinions: "It is immediately obvious that one of the emotionally satisfying aspects of Gundam is the way in which children pilot these huge and powerful mechanical warriors. Therefore they can deliver to children what many other successful children's books and films have done—feelings of power.

"But the feelings that are produced in your work are far more complex. I think of the way in which individuals are cut off from society, isolated within these suits. Do these readings of the imagery make any sense to you?

"Naturally, I think of children and trauma of war, of their inherent powerlessness. One then can see these suits as offering a protection that is never available in the horrors of real-life war.

"I look at the sculpture of Kenji Yanobe and see individuals enclosed within postapocalyptic survival vehicles. I wonder if you know Mr. Yanobe's work and if you feel any connection with it? You were both children when the atomic bombs were dropped, when Tokyo was firebombed. Could you comment on this?"

By the time Charley and I got to Japan, I was also coming to see the Mobile Suits as a metaphor for a curiously elusive personality type called an *otaku.* An otaku is often described as someone who lives alone in a small room and connects with the world only via computer. Of course, this touched on my own concerns about my son and the cell phone, my son and the ticket machines, my son and the Destructor Simulator, please insert two tokens.

As it happens, the first time Charley and I encountered the term was in the glossary of the show at the Brooklyn Museum: "Otaku: an anime fan. The term literally means 'you' in a very formal sense. In Japan, it has come to mean people who are obsessed with something to the point where they have few personal relationships. The nature of the obsession can be anything from anime to computers. In Japan otaku has the same negative connotation as nerd. In America, however, it refers specifically to hardcore anime fans, without any negative connotations."

Yet no definition of otaku was ever completely satisfying and by the time we left Japan, I had asked perhaps twenty people to define it for me; few of them agreed, and some answers were more disturbing than others.

This is an excellent example of how perplexing Japanese culture can be, and a reminder of why Kosei Ono's warning is worth heeding. Better to know nothing than a little, for the more you try to pin down *otaku*, the more wriggly it gets. Lawrence Eng, the author of *The Politics of Otaku*, comments that *otaku* means, literally, "your house," and more generally is a distant, formal way of saying "you." Later he suggests the term originated amongst the collectors of animation pictures. "The basic idea," he writes, "is that the word is used to explicitly indicate detachedness from who you are speaking to. For example, a dedicated and experienced collector of cels [the transparent plastic sheets on which animators paint] will have a vast network of connections to aid in his or her search for rare cels." These contacts would be at once familiar and far from intimate.

But as so often is the case in the Japanese language, just when you think you may almost understand a word, hopeless complications destroy it anew. In the late eighties a man named Tsutomu Miyazaki kidnapped and murdered four little girls and the police found his apartment crammed with anime and manga and videos, some of them pornographic. From this time the word *otaku* became associated with sociopaths, serial killers.

In an article written with his colleague Timothy Blum, my New York friend the sculptor Jon Kessler complicates it further: "*Otaku* are the generations of kids raised to memorize volumes of contextless information for university entrance exams. Somewhere a glitch occurred and they are stuck in information mode, hoarding and exchanging information about the seemingly useless obsessions of *otaku*, such as the bra sizes of idols, to information about Levi's 501 jeans, as well as secrets about their mischievous break-ins to data-banks. . . . *Otaku*s are socially inept information junkies who rarely leave their homes, preferring to interface with the world via data-banks, modems and faxes."

And what about my own dear son? Well, back in Sega World his face was washed by flashing red lights as he let off another twenty rounds, fighting street to street.

"Enough," I said. "Let's go."

But he was stuck to the machine. "One more, please."

"No. You need to rest. You've got Kabuki tomorrow."

"No, you promised! No Real Japan!"

"This is not the real Japan. This is something else."

"What is it then? You don't know," said Charley desperately. He nodded to Takashi who, it seemed, had been standing behind me all this time. "Ask him."

"Can I help you, Carey-san?"

"I was trying to explain to Charley about Kabuki."

"Ah," he said, "yes, my grandmother likes Kabuki."

Later I understood: he was dying of embarrassment for my son, but at the time I could not read the curious rictus on the Gundam pilot's face.

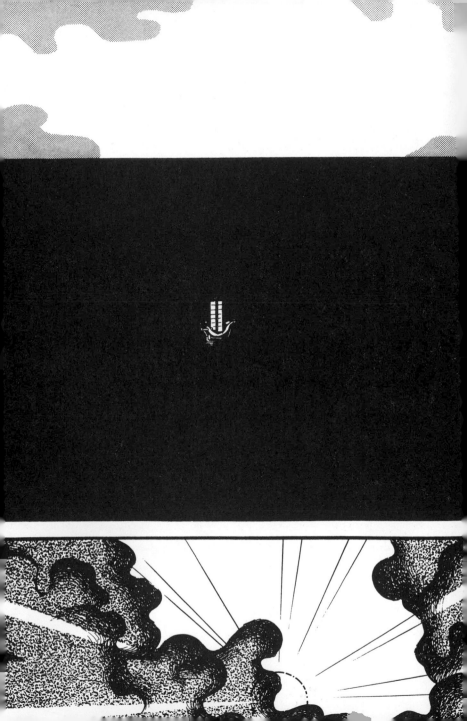

4.

Charley squirmed and whined. He had no idea what Kabuki was, only that he'd hate it, and it was not only Kabuki that produced this visceral response but the whiff of culture in any form. To see his face that night in our hotel room, you would've thought I was commanding him to drink molten lead. In both New York and London, he had happily attended shows of contemporary Japanese art, and we'd found ourselves, amazingly, in agreement about what we liked. But Kabuki was in another category and that it meant "crooked" or "deviant" failed to calm him down.

"Last night," he said, "you told me it meant the song-and-dance art."

"Well, that's another meaning."

"Dad, you don't really know. Stop pretending that you do."

"Okay, but we're still going. Now go to sleep."

He woke me at 3 a.m., pleading to be spared, even offering to do chores at home to pay me back for the tickets.

In the spooky light from the street I could see his contorted face, the Gundam figures standing guard all around the room, the glowing face of the cell phone.

"Kabuki," I said, "is like the manga of its time."

"No it isn't."

"Then go to sleep."

There was so much more I might have said, but it was pointless. It certainly wouldn't have helped to quote to him from Alex Kerr's sad and celebratory book, *Lost Japan*, where, in his chapter on Kabuki, he writes: "Focus on the 'instant' is characteristic of Japanese culture as a whole. In Chinese poetry, the poet's imagination might begin with flowers and rivers, and then suddenly leap up into the Nine Heavens to ride a dragon to Mt. K'un-lun and frolic with the immortals. Japanese haiku focus on the mundane moment, as in Bashō's well-known poem: The old pond, a frog leaps in, the sound of water."

You can see this as a frame from a manga.

And there are other connections and parallels. In Kabuki, he writes, "There might be a scene where two people are casually talking; then, from some detail in the conversation, the characters suddenly comprehend each other's true feelings. In that instant, action stops, actors freeze, and from stage left wooden clappers go *battari*! The two characters resume speaking as though nothing has happened; however, in the instant of that *battari*!, everything has changed. While most forms of theater try to preserve a narrative continuity, Kabuki focuses around such crucial instants of stop and start, start and stop."

Just like manga!

But none of these amazing insights would ease the anguish of my son, who, at one o'clock the following afternoon, made his way through the crowd of straight-backed grandmothers, many of them dressed formally in kimonos. He was a miserable

American boy with leather bands around his wrist and a homemade T-shirt that read GEORGE BUSH, NOT MY PRESIDENT. He entered the auditorium of the famous Kabukiza as cheerfully as Gonpachi, a character in one of the plays we were about to see, was delivered to his own execution.

"Sit up."

"No."

And he did not yet know the performance would be four hours long! As he said to me later, "How could you do that to me?"

Yes, I'd broken my promise about the Real Japan. But I'd foolishly hoped he might somehow become interested in an art form which once had been as disreputable as manga was today. After all, Kabuki was considered so deviant that it had been banished up the river to Yoshiwara, although the actual nature of the Yoshiwara Pleasure Gardens was not something I wished to discuss with my son in any detail.

"There's a fighting scene," I said. "With ladders."

"Great."

Bored and restless, the poor boy endured play after play, expecting each one to be the last. And while I could not possibly admit it to him, I was not always fully engaged either. Yet there was one play,

Sono Kouta Yume mo Yoshiwara, we both liked, and even though Charley now insists all this is entirely my own invention, I remember how he stilled as his attention was seized.

Gonpachi is brought to the execution site on horseback, then pulled off the horse. A severe official dolefully recites the details of his crimes before asking him if there is any last statement he wishes to make. This being Kabuki, Gonpachi naturally wishes to speak, launching into a long and passionate confession. Born into a good samurai family, he had committed a murder in a moment of passion and fled to Edo. Then, in Yoshiwara, he fell in love with a geisha. Now, everyone understands that such affairs are an expensive business, so he had fallen into debt and from there to robbery.

He now repents and asks everyone to pray for his soul.

The geisha arrives as the speech ends, having slipped away from Yoshiwara to say good-bye. Beautiful, pitiful, she begs the officials to let her share a drink of water with her lover, and one of them relents. Only then does the geisha reveal that she has a knife. My foreigner's heart leaps with hope when she cuts the ropes binding Gonpachi, but then the guards rush in. Gonpachi struggles to defend himself, warding off the guards' staves in such a way that they make a cross, an echo of the crucifix on which he is condemned to die.

In the second act we discover that all of this had been a terrifying dream. Gonpachi had fallen asleep in a palanquin, and now wakes to find himself in the Yoshiwara Pleasure Gardens. What an enormous relief! I had inhabited his remorse, felt the merciless weight of Tokugawa law, but now the gardens are so beautiful, so bright, so alive with flowers. It is the very opposite of the Western tradition where the hero dies in the last frame after merely dreaming of a happy life.

Now a letter from the geisha is delivered, in which she begs him to hurry to her side, and so off he goes—one more leaf drifting on the waters of the floating world. The program notes explain that his happiness is overlaid with a certain gloom, but I was left refreshed and delighted, wondering if the brothels of Yoshiwara could have really been so beautiful.

Charley denounced the experience as the worst four hours of his entire life, even worse than when he cut his heel on a broken bottle and received his stitches under inadequate anaesthetic. He, however, was the one who later brought up the subject of Yoshiwara. Was it still there? Could we see it?

I would have loved to visit the Yoshiwara of the Genroku era, which Howard Hibbett describes so

eloquently in *The Floating World in Japanese Fiction*.
Here, in a luxurious setting, merchants and suffi-
ciently prosperous samurai enjoyed sparkling, viva-
cious company that could be found nowhere else in
Japan. The chief pleasure quarters—the Shimabara
in Kyoto, the Edo Yoshiwara, and the Osaka Shim-
machi—were made up of large groups of buildings,
some of them magnificent, which served as the fine
restaurants, the exclusive clubs, the leading salons of
the day. Not least were the great "teahouses," as
brothels were often called, where famous courtesans
joined the candlelit banquets and parties given by
men of fashion. One such house, the Sumiya, in the
Shimabara, still stands and has been designated an
Important Cultural Property. This establishment is
not only a handsome and spacious one, from its
reception hall to its vast kitchen, it is also in the best
of taste: a delightful garden, sliding panels decorated
by the foremost painters, a distinctive screen pattern
and style of metal fittings for each room. The general effect is chaste and aristocratic, rather than
voluptuous or rococo. Despite my son's worldly
comments about "entertainment districts," I judged
it best to withhold these fascinating details.

"It's all gone," I answered him. "Bombed
flat during the war—Yoshiwara, and Asakusa, and
Ueno, too."

What I didn't tell him was that Yoshiwara had been in severe decline long before the war, and that what had once been the subject of plays, novels, and Hokusai woodcuts had by now become a district of gangs and massage parlours.

In 1939 Yoshiwara boasted three hundred and twenty brothels. When the firebombing was over, only ten were left standing. The American army of occupation swiftly established Special Recreation centres in the few unbombed factories, and price lists were posted on the quartermaster bulletin boards: *20 yen—a buck and a quarter—for the first hour. 10 yen for each additional hour and all night for 50 yen. If you pay more, you spoil it for the rest. The MP's will be stationed at the doors to enforce these prices. Trucks will leave here each hour, on the hour. NO MATTER HOW GOOD IT FEELS, BE SURE TO WEAR ONE.*

"He'd be sad," said Charley, as if reading my thoughts.

"Who?"

"What's-his-name. Gonpachi?"

"Yes," I said. "He would."

5.

It is Hiroshima and Nagasaki that we Westerners remember, somehow obliterating from our collective memory the firebombing not only of working-class Shitamachi but of the more upscale Yamanote and, finally, of all Tokyo, a catastrophe movingly dramatized in *Grave of the Fireflies*, one of the most powerful anime yet produced. The director, Isao Takahata, is the business partner of the much more famous director Hayao Miyazaki, whose work includes *Princess Mononoke* and *Spirited Away*, but *Grave of the Fireflies*, the story of a teenage boy, Seita, and his little sister, Setsuko, is equal to any of Miyazaki's great films. Seita and Setsuko's father is serving in the navy, so when their mother is killed in the firebombing they are abandoned in a burning world. At first they stay with their aunt, but she is so lacking in affection, so loudly resentful of the expense of housing them, that they decide to look out for themselves, living in a cave by a stream. What starts as playing house becomes more and more serious as Seita is reduced to stealing in order to feed his sister. Ultimately, he cannot look after her and she dies of malnutrition. Seita painfully makes his way back to the devastated Tokyo, where he becomes yet another lost child and dies in a crowded railway station.

It was this film that led us to our meeting with Mr. Yazaki, not because he was an animator—he was not—but because he had been Charley's age at the time of the firebombing. This was really all I knew about the very pleasant, very articulate Mr. Yazaki. I never questioned him about his life as an adult, a writer, an intellectual, and never, in fact, understood how he might know my agent, Paul Hulbert, or exactly what chain of relationships had persuaded him to talk about these few months of childhood to an untidy Australian about whom he, in turn, must have known almost nothing.

He was a story; I was a writer; and that was our relationship. If I use only his family name it is because I cannot translate the first name on his business card.

"My friend," said Mr. Yazaki, "is the novelist who wrote *Grave of the Fireflies*, the novel on which the film is based. Not surprisingly, there are some points of connection between his life and the novel. For instance, he was evacuated to Kobe during the war while his sister stayed in Tokyo. She was killed in the firebombing, and all throughout his life—he's three years older than I am—he has felt guilty that he was not in Tokyo to help her. Perhaps this affected the novel.

"My own experiences," said Mr. Yazaki, "were different, but there are some points of similarity, as you'll see.

"The normal Japanese school year starts in April, but 1944 was not normal, and after only a month my class was evacuated from Tokyo, the whole sixth grade, to Nagaoka.

"Was I afraid? Not at all. I was about Charley's age. I was with my teachers, classmates, all my best friends. We were living in a Buddhist temple. And perhaps you don't know this, Carey-san, but in Japanese culture, a temple or shrine is considered a sanctuary for children. No one bothered with air-raid drills. Why would we have needed them?

"It was one of those perfect summer days right at the end of the rainy season. We swam in the river and chased dragonflies. Back at the temple, we had our dinner and then a bath and we were just getting down to our homework when the first bomb dropped. It wasn't like you think—no whistle, no big bang, just a noise like very heavy rain. You were talking about *Grave of the Fireflies*. Well, it was like that. These were incendiary bombs, and suddenly the whole world caught on fire.

"Though we had no training, we were like schoolchildren on a class trip. We behaved like a class, and this is why we had no injuries or loss of life. There were five adults with us, and they led us out of the temple and up the hill. We looked back down and saw our temple burning, all the houses around it too.

"We stayed shivering in the woods all that night, and when it got light we stayed there, waiting for the fires to stop. We were hungry, but when we came out of the forest there was nothing left, nothing to eat, nowhere to sleep. There was nothing to do but go back to Tokyo.

"I often think: If we had not been bombed, we

would have lived in Nagaoka all through the war; I would never have experienced the Tokyo bombing on March 10 the following year. A third of the children I knew were killed, but they would still be alive.

"I came home to Setagaya-ku—that's in the Yamanote district, in the southwest of Tokyo. My mother was living there, also my younger sister, and my father, who was never conscripted by the military. He was a publisher, and his company had been ordered to produce reading material for the armed forces.

"No, he wasn't involved in manga, although it's true that manga was used as propaganda by the army.

"Now that I was home, I could go back to my original school, but all my old teachers were in the army. As a matter of fact, I didn't go to school too often. Everyone was expecting a big air raid on Tokyo. I was often told it was too dangerous to use the train. The Americans had retaken Saipan and Guam, so they no longer needed aircraft carriers to launch attacks on our country. Their air supremacy was complete.

"You might think I had some happy moments in all of this. I was only twelve years old, after all, but you have to remember I had already been bombed once. What I remember is that we had lots of air-raid training. It was a tense, anxious time. When sirens went off in the middle of the night, we would rush into the shelter in our backyard.

"There were plenty of air raids during the next nine months, all targeted at bases and ordnance factories. But then, on March 10, the Americans decided to bomb Shitamachi. You know what I mean? Downtown, where you are staying now. Asakusa, Ueno, the working-class area of Tokyo—also the most densely populated. The houses in Shitamachi were very close together, the families big.

"The bombing began at eight o'clock at night. And although it was quite a distance away from us, the noise was enormous and the sky was red all night.

"We lived in a traditional two-storey Japanese house with a tiled roof and drainpipes, so it was no great difficulty for me and my friends to climb up the drainpipe and sit on the roof—and from there we had a very good view of the bombing. As I said, the Americans had already destroyed anything which could have fired back at them, so now they owned the sky. Some of their aircraft were fitted with powerful searchlights so they could illuminate their targets. The scene looked very frightening, but it was exciting too.

"My parents didn't know where I was and they were worried, but then they heard us shouting, *Look, there's another one! Look at that!* It took them a long time to understand that we were on the roof. Then they got really angry. You see, the Americans had low-flying fighters and if they'd seen us they'd have strafed us. Naturally, I got a hiding.

"Officially, one hundred twenty thousand people died in that raid, but there were really a million victims if you count everyone who lost a home or was injured or orphaned. You were in New York, Charley, when the terrorists struck the World Trade Center. Three thousand people died, and that was an enormous number. You know what that was like, so now imagine what one hundred twenty thousand is like.

"The next day we saw the first of the people fleeing from downtown. But the traffic went both ways. People from Yamanote went to Shitamachi with food and blankets. We had downtown friends who came to live with us. Still, all our friends who survived were also victims, because they had lost a parent, or both parents, or a brother or sister, and if they wanted to go back to downtown they often couldn't reach their destination. Shitamachi was burning and burning and burning.

"After this raid, my younger sister was evacuated to a city called Mito, northeast of Tokyo, where my mother's mother lived.

"As for me, I was twelve and therefore was expected to work in an ordnance factory. I was sent to a place in Mikawa—on the Arakawa River, in Shitamachi—I guess you would call it a foundry. They melted scrap iron and poured it into ingots and reused it for weapons, guns, bombs. So they'd bring in loads of scrap iron from the bombed buildings, and my job was to separate the iron from the less useful metals. Most of my day was spent carrying heavy metal from one place to another. Since I had no idea what I was doing, I made many mistakes.

"There were a number of home-guard soldiers who supervised the work and decided on punishments. You have to remember that it was an age of militarism, so if you made a little mistake you were punished immediately and severely.

"To be honest, I didn't mind being hit. What was worse, they often punished everyone for one person's error. For instance, everyone might have to go without a meal. They were hungry times anyway, and missing a dinner was very difficult. Sometimes they'd make everyone work another couple of hours, which was probably less cruel than it sounds now. We children had been brainwashed into thinking that we were 'citizens-in-waiting,' about to go out and fight for our country. So we were mentally prepared for this treatment.

"Then the factory was attacked.

"We heard the air-raid warning and rushed outside. We were used to seeing fighter planes. They always accompanied the bombers, but in this case there were only fighters. Though we thought the target was the factory, it was the workers they wanted. And as we ran across the rough ground to the riverbank, they already had us in their sights. They came in so low we could see the pilots' faces as they strafed us. A few hours before I'd been eating with these boys and men, working and joking with them, but now my friends' flesh was flying through the air, ripped apart by machine-gun bullets. Twenty of us escaped to the banks of the Arakawa. Seven of us died. This would have had a profound effect on a grown man, but on a twelve-year-old boy, I cannot describe the shock. If you don't mind, I'd rather not discuss this anymore.

"I know that on the night of the big bombing raid on Shitamachi, my parents had been anxious that Yamanote would soon suffer. For a while I thought they had been wrong, but on May 25 it happened. As before, it was at eight o'clock.

"Once again I would hear that sound like heavy rain, and since each incendiary is like a number of bombs, when one hits the ground you don't know where it's going to explode. You see this very clearly in *Grave of the Fireflies.* It's all around you. In a situation like this, people don't grab hold of each other's hands and hide together. They look out for themselves. The first set of planes drops its bombs, then a second lot drop more bombs, and maybe you choose to hide under a tree in a park. If you're lucky, no firebomb falls on that tree and you survive. But there's no logic that tells you where to go to hide. You could have chosen a tree at the other side of the park and you'd be dead.

"The irony of it is that our house wasn't hit at all during the bombing. If we had stayed there, we wouldn't have seen the horrors we did.

"Until the night of a Yamanote firebombing, my family were resigned to the fact that I would go to fight. Now they had seen war with their own eyes, all they could think of was finding me somewhere safe to hide.

"At the beginning of June, my mother took me to a city in Yamanashi Prefecture. Kofu was a resort, completely surrounded by mountains, one of which is Fuji. In Kofu, my father thought, it would be impossible to be attacked from the air. The bombers would have to go over and between mountains, down into this basin. So my mother bought a house there and we lived there together. Given my father's important role in propaganda, no one insisted that I continue to work in a factory. In any case, there were very few factories left.

"July 7 is the day of the festival of Tanabata—you write a wish on paper and you tie it to a piece of bamboo. I can't remember what I wished for, but it certainly was not what happened on that night.

"Apparently the American air force had planned to attack Niigata with B29 bombers but then they discovered that the weather was bad, so they attacked Kofu instead. Though Niigata is a big industrial port town, all Kofu had was one factory manufacturing aircraft parts and one very small garrison of elite special forces. Somehow these soldiers knew, even before the sirens sounded, that the bombers were coming. So they ran away, leaving the rest of us completely undefended. On that day I understood that the army was not there to protect people after all.

"It's not so much the sirens I remember as the lights. The Americans had been able to land forces and set up huge searchlights on a hill above the town. One minute it was a lovely silky Tanabata night, next thing we were less than insects, the whole town caught in a blinding white light.

"Our house was on the very edge of the town with nothing but rice paddies for neighbours, so I ran to where there were no buildings worth bombing. In all the panic, I was separated from my mother, but we'd been looking after this younger kid—he'd lost his parents in the Tokyo attack. This little boy trusted me, depended on me, so there was no question I had to protect him. I even waited while he gathered up toys, carrying them with him as we ran out into the dark. As for my toys, I lost them all.

"We stayed together in the rice paddies until the Americans had destroyed Kofu. Since the town was small, it took only two or three hours until no building remained.

"When I made my wish on Tanabata, three hundred thousand people were living in Kofu. Next morning, one hundred thousand of them were dead. You cannot imagine what it was like to go back. The streets were full of dead bodies and we had to walk over them. Many were still burning, and you could see their smouldering red-pink flesh. There were people who died standing up, completely charred and dead.

"And I thought that it was no longer a matter of winning a war or losing a war. This was the end of the world, or even worse. Maybe hell was something like this.

"I couldn't go back to Tokyo, because it was being bombed every night. Obviously, I couldn't stay in Kofu because there was nothing left. So my mother decided to send me to Mito, where my sister was, and then she went back to Tokyo to be with my father.

"This was when I wished I had died in the first air raid, so I would not have had to experience all these terrible things. However, I went to Mito, where I would be safe—and guess what happened?

"Three days before the end of the war, Mito was shelled by the American navy. Fortunately, my grandmother's house was very close to the coast, so the shells passed overhead. But the noise was horrific. It felt like an earthquake and the earthquake was happening every second. The house shook and shuddered. There were pauses in the shelling, though never a pause we could calculate. We'd think it was all over, and begin dinner again, but then it would start and go on and on and on. We knew why they were shelling us. They were getting ready to land their troops.

"I went to school most days. We spent our time making bamboo spears we could use to kill the American soldiers when they invaded. Because our school was about an hour and a half from my grandmother's place, I was sometimes too frightened to come home alone and often spent the night at school.

"Suddenly, on August 1, the ships disappeared from the coast. It was a very quiet, peaceful time.

Then, on August 15 the war ended. This current prime minister is too young to know anything about the war, so this is why he feels he can visit the shrine of the army's war dead, and why he thinks we should change the constitution so Japan can have an army once again.

"When I talk to young people, they all say war is bad, war is frightening, but if you ask if they would defend their country, they all say yes. This attitude is very different from mine.

"How about you, Carey-san, I don't suppose you experienced the war?"

"Not really, Mr. Yazaki, but I do remember playing with Japanese army occupation money as a child."

Mr. Yazaki was silent a moment. I had no idea what he was feeling.

"I am thinking," he offered, "about the people in Afghanistan, Kosovo, Palestine, and I think about how it is for those children. We read a book called *A Farewell to Arms*, but when will we finally say good-bye to them?"

6.

Heart of Animation
Beats in a Robot Boy

By James Brooke

TOKYO, April 6—Back in 1951, Osamu Tezuka, a Japanese cartoonist, dreamed up Astro
Boy, a lovable robot with laser fingertips,
search-light eyes, machine guns in his black

shorts, and rocket jets flaming from his red boots.

To make the 100,000 horsepower tyke seem really futuristic, the artist gave his creation a truly far-out birth date: April 7, 2003.

Tokyo may not yet have flying cars, but Astro Boy's official birthday on Monday marks the coming of age of Japan's animation industry. No longer marginalized, the bare-chested rocket boy with the spiky hair, known in Japanese as Tetsuwan Atom [literally Iron-Arm Atom] is being hailed with fireworks, costume parades, intellectual seminars, an exhibit in Parliament and a $1 million diamond-and-ruby likeness in a downtown department store display.

"We Japanese want to live alongside robots, that is why we love Astro Boy," said Takao Imai, a 72 year old lawyer, dressed in a white smock and a white wig of cotton curls to look like Professor Elefun, Astro Boy's eccentric scientist protector.

This appeared in the *New York Times* well after our return from Tokyo, but that quote—*we Japanese want to live alongside robots*—recalled again this common but inexplicable enthusiasm.

At first I had been tempted to regard the robot as a kind of mechanised Godzilla, a metaphor for the technological might of the atomic bomb. This, however, was undercut by my discovery of a wild and terrifying cartoon produced two years before Hiroshima, titled *Kagaku Senshi Nyū Yōku ni Shutsugen su* ("The Science Warrior Appears in New York"). In it, a giant robot with vast spiked feet stamps flat the buildings on Manhattan whilst it puffs steam or smoke or poison from every hinge and hole of its Tin Man body. Though the bomb could not explain the robot, one cannot escape the impotent rage, and even obsession, that the image conjures up. When Commodore Perry broke through the wall that had surrounded Japan for two hundred years, he perhaps engendered passions suggested by the robot, but I kept this notion to myself. Because once I was in Japan, I understood that, as a foreigner, I could never know the truth.

Certainly I saw the effects of World War II in almost every anime we watched, in the continually crumbling cities, in those ever-present preternaturally powerful children who threatened to obliterate the universe, and most particularly in the series Mobile Suit Gundam, whose creator we set off to meet one sunny summer's day. We were accompanied by my friend from the English Agency, Paul Hulbert and—this was a complete surprise—Takashi, who appeared from behind a newsstand near Asakusa Station. My son immediately brightened.

"Charley, did you invite him?"

"Dad, please. You don't know what this means to him."

I looked at Takashi. His tension was palpable, his cheeks a heightened rosy colour. He smiled at me, although what that meant I could not guess.

"But we haven't asked Mr. Tomino," I told my son as we boarded the subway. "This interview has taken months to arrange. They're very formal about all this."

Poor Takashi was not insensitive to my feelings. On the train he stood a little apart, very erect in his bearing.

"He won't ask questions, Dad. He just wants to come. Don't be so mean. Mr. Tomino is his hero."

I saw his point. If Charley had endured Kabuki for me, I could handle whatever ripples Takashi's presence might cause. Having resolved that he should come, I was surprised again when, during the short walk from Kichijoji Station to Sunrise Studios, he vanished.

It is the nature of tourism that one returns not only with trinkets and postcards but also with memories of misunderstandings, hurts ignorantly inflicted across the borderlines of language and custom. At Kichijoji Station, it seemed I had acquired one more. As it turned out, however, Takashi Ko, second lieutenant of the third battalion, was simply unable to confront his creator. Still, the bad taste lingers: social anxiety had made me less generous than I should have been.

Sunrise Studios occupies an office building of no particular charm, and it was not until we entered the second-floor studio that we met the twelve-foot-high plastic robot. Here, at last, I saw my son's face take on that complete and utter blankness which reveals his deepest secret pleasures. Who could believe we were here? Which of his friends would even believe it possible?

We were led into a meeting room where we were seven in all, one boy and six men, most notably Yoshiyuki Tomino himself, a youthful sixty years of age, slim, balding, with large eyeglasses and that curious combination often seen in artists, an obvious sensitivity linked with a paradoxically unbending will.

My friend Paul brought to the table not only extraordinary fluency in Japanese, a highly educated literary sensibility, but also an intimate familiarity with manga.

In addition, there was Irie-san, a senior editor of Kodansha, the giant publishing firm that produced much of the printed material, some of it physically immense, generated by Mobile Suit Gundam. He was a man with an untidy mop of hair and such obvious kindness and intelligence that it was with him more than anyone I met that I felt my lack of language most acutely.

There were also two Sunrise executives whose cards I have, typically but regretfully, since lost. For some doubtless simple reason, everyone at this meeting was Mr., never san.

Charley had bought one of Mr. Tomino's books to be autographed and he gravely, gracefully obliged, choosing a large fat gold pen. There would be a price for this.

"So you like Gundam?" Mr. Tomino asked in English.

"Yes."

This, in my son's view, was payment enough. But Mr. Tomino was pressing him like a fifth-grade teacher. What exactly had Charley liked about Mobile Suit Gundam?

Six pairs of adult eyes were on him.

"I like the story line," he admitted, "and how it's complicated." He paused. Mr. Tomino nodded encouragingly. Three tape recorders turned. "The characters are complicated too," he said, then turned to me for help.

I asked Mr. Tomino when he had thought of making an anime or manga.

As I spoke, Japanese translations of questions

I'd submitted prior to the meeting—most of which I had by now forgotten—were being passed around the table.

Mr. Tomino lowered his eyes and began to speak in a soft, musical voice which seemed, to my ear, at variance with his animated manner.

"Mr. Tomino doesn't even want to make an anime now," Paul translated in a very English-sounding English that gave no indication of his Greek blood or his Japanese life. "Mr. Tomino," he said, "just wants to make films."

Mr. Tomino moved the sheet containing my questions a few inches to the left and then spoke for a minute or two.

"Gundam was launched just to sell toy robots," said Paul at last, "to create a product that people would buy. There is no real inspiration behind it. He made Gundam because it was his job to make Gundam. And before Gundam, he made lots of animations which were also used to advertise robot toys."

If Charley was disappointed by this news, he did not reveal it.

Mr. Tomino explained further, and Paul conveyed the explanation: "You see, Mr. Tomino was also very interested in science fiction, so he wanted to make something that was like a movie and that could incorporate these robots. That was his job.

But when he was asked to make Gundam, the only condition he had was that the robot should be twenty metres tall. Then the toy makers wanted him to have a one-hundred-metre robot."

I wondered if that was a good thing or a bad thing but missed my chance to ask.

"That," said Paul, "gave Mr. Tomino a logical problem. A hundred-metre robot would be very heavy."

"Too heavy," Mr. Tomino said in English.

"If it was to stand and walk on a normal asphalt road," Paul explained, "that was a problem. There was another problem: the toy makers wanted to set the story on Earth, but Mr. Tomino wanted it in space."

"In the universe," insisted Mr. Tomino.

"But the toy makers were adamant," Paul soon translated. "They needed the planet Earth, they said, in order to show how huge the robot was. So Mr. Tomino compromised. He created the Space Colony, which had mountains and rivers and things that were of more earthly scale. But not even that was enough, so in the end he was forced to bring Gundam to Earth. Of course he was resistant—in Mr. Tomino's mind, the Mobile Suits were things that couldn't work, couldn't even move on this planet."

What did all this mean to Mr. Tomino? It was impossible to guess. In any case, he slid my list of questions back a few inches to the right. In the original English, my second question had read: "Charley and I were always interested in watching Mobile Suit Gundam. However, we continually wondered what we were missing. What might be obvious to a Japanese viewer but inaccessible to us?"

Mr. Tomino closed his eyes and made a long *mmmmmmm* sound before he answered.

"There is nothing you are missing," Paul translated, "and the reason is that Mr. Tomino made sure there wouldn't be anything like that at all. For instance, he tried to avoid having ethnicity, and so he replaced *common sense,* which is based on culture, with *general sense,* which is a kind of universal sense that all human beings have."

Huh?

"Mr. Tomino tried to remove all cultural elements."

"Perhaps," I suggested, "he is being universal in a Japanese way."

Mr. Tomino was nice enough to laugh.

"But when a character speaks," I insisted, "and they speak the Japanese language, surely the *way* they speak must communicate some social value? If so, we foreigners can't hear that. Might a character's voice not suggest a place of birth or a level of education?"

"Ahhhhh." said Mr. Tomino, as if I had understood nothing.

"Mr. Tomino thinks," said Paul, "that there is maybe something in your own character which is interested in national identity. As for Mr. Tomino, he has avoided it completely. He has always tried to make his characters as standard and as universal as possible by *not* giving them local colour or national colour or ethnic colour."

"I suspect Mr. Tomino will disagree," I said, "but there is no escaping the fact that you have invented a big war story, and that type of story affects children's emotions a great deal. On one side of the equation, you give them a sense of power. When they vicariously become Gundam pilots, they have great might. But when they are children in a war, they are terrified, if not traumatised forever."

"Well," Mr. Tomino explained through Paul, "in order to have a story that would involve the toy maker's products, the suits and the weapons, it was necessary to have a story involving armies. And if you have armies and weapons then you need to have battles.

"And then the toy manufacturers wanted the characters to be children, because children will buy the toys. But it is true," Paul interpreted, "that the theme of having the battlefield and children is a very interesting one for Mr. Tomino. He can remember something about World War II and of course he heard stories from his father and his father's friends.

At that time in Japan you had to go to military academy when you were sixteen, to war when you were seventeen. Boys became adults between the ages of thirteen and fifteen. Also, you must remember there had been samurai who fought on the battlefields when they were as young as thirteen.

"Thinking about it historically," our interpreter continued, "there is nothing very unusual about having such young boys taking part in a war. In fact, the last two world wars were the first major conflicts where children did not fight. Perhaps that was a mistake made by adults."

"How do you mean?"

"Being able to fight in a war is an expression of one's citizenship. If you are an adult, you do it as a responsible citizen. But if you are a child—these days, I mean—war makes you either a victim or an accomplice."

This was getting way too Japanese for me. I told Mr. Tomino I did not quite get this point.

" 'Victim' and 'accomplice' both have to do with crime, but 'citizenship' has to do with public duty and responsibility."

This reply shocked me a little, but delighted me too. Here, after all, was evidence of the intensely different cultural view Charley and I had suspected was buried deep in anime. Here was all the good stuff Mr. Tomino had told me did not exist.

"You see," Paul translated again, "in the time since World War II, we've completely forgotten what happens to children during wartime and the parts they have played. So Mr. Tomino has no qualms at all about having children in a fighting role in the story. That's how it's been throughout history. The public responsibility, the responsibility of all citizens, is very great."

"It's a burden," Paul said, and I was briefly confused as to whether he was translating or giving his own opinion. "And that's something he wanted to include in Gundam. At the same time, when the children put on the Mobile Suits it's not something that's cool and logical and rational—it's when a child becomes a hero. It has to do with glory and it has to do with honour."

"Japan," I said, "has been a society in which honour plays an important role. Would Tomino agree that this actually makes Gundam very Japanese?"

"Yes."

"Also," I suggested, "if you're Japanese and watching Gundam, you will think about samurai more than once?"

"No."

"No?" I asked, incredulous.

Mr. Tomino closed his eyes and shook his head.

Now I regret not introducing Takashi to him, and also that I did not ask how, for God's sake, he could say that Gundam Mobile Suits are not *exactly* like samurai. But I had reached that point that can arrive easily in an interpreted interview—locked inside my skin, lost in space, emotionally disconnected from my fellow humans.

The interview, of course, continued.

To Takashi, waiting on the street outside, it must have seemed forever.

7.

Not so far from the ancient temple of Gokokuji we met our first real otaku. Yuka Minakawa was an attractive, gym-toned young woman in a yellow dress and fuck-me heels who came clicking so sexily toward us across Kodansha's banklike foyer. Could this be an otaku? Yes, absolutely. Could it be a woman? I didn't think so. I glanced at Charley.

"It's okay," he said. "I get it."

"Are you cool?"

"Dad, we live in the West Village."

As our eccentric little party crossed the foyer, Charley looked at me poker-faced and said: "Finally, the Real Japan."

Of course to think that manga and transsexual otakus are somehow more authentic than temples is wrongheaded, but this actually was *our* Japan, and we liked it here.

We passed a room of suited men gravely considering a toy robot on a conference table. In another room, Charley and I were presented with an encyclopedic book titled *Gundam Officials, Limited Edition.* To say this was as large as a telephone book severely understates the case, for it weighed almost seven pounds, concrete evidence of the otaku mindset and an extreme consequence, perhaps, of an education system based on the accumulation and memorization of data.

My son, I knew, would never surrender the gift. I was doomed to lug it home across the world, this gorgeously produced, very expensive tome in which every known fact about Mobile Suit Gundam was carefully documented and illustrated, with the sort of respect you might expect in the owner's manual for a Rolex Rocket Ship. It was the Real Japan, and we could not read a word of it.

Now we gathered in another conference room, and here we were invited to ask Yuka, the author of this bible, anything we liked. Charley, as usual, was reluctant to speak, but when I replayed the audiotapes back in New York—hearing myself ask Yuka: What was this thing with robots? What was an otaku?—I wondered how difficult it would be for an outsider to recognise that my son was the author of my questions.

Paul translated Yuka's reply, which, on the tape at home, was still delicate and careful but much more male than I had noticed at the time. "In the middle eighties, there was a Japanese science-fiction author called Moto Arai. One of her stylistic tics was to address the reader very formally with the second person pronoun, otaku, a much more distant form than the French *vous,* for instance. Her fans liked this book so much that they adopted this peculiar usage, referring to each other as 'otaku.' "

I had read enough to imagine that I understood. "Isn't it an extremely respectful form of address?" I asked.

"No!" Yuka cried in English.

Charley's eyes flicked my way.

"The way 'otaku' is used now," Paul translated, "it's the reverse. It is no longer about fans imitating Moto Arai's prose. It's not fun anymore. It's not respectful, it's discriminatory. It's like calling you 'sir' when I don't really mean it. It's ironic, sarcastic."

Okay, so the word's *dripping* with discrimination. "But doesn't it have a number of meanings?"

"Of course," Paul said. "It can be used for people who are enthusiastic about almost anything. In English you might say *aficionado,* although it is also rather like *nerd.*"

In the midst of this explanation, the staff of Kodansha, so earnestly at work only minutes previously, erupted into wild cheering. Yuka did not blink an eye. And although sararimen in offices all over Tokyo had abandoned their posts to watch Japan battle Tunisia, she was far more interested in drawing a fat teenager with a schlumpy T-shirt and a bad complexion.

"Otaku," she said, pushing it across the table.

"As you can see," Paul said, "in this sense an otaku is someone who has no dress or social sense or any interest in anything other than the object of their obsession. This may or may not be manga. It could easily be the bra sizes of actresses."

Yuka interrupted and Paul translated: "Also, among the otaku community there are many of us who will laugh and make fun of this sort of person. We used to have a badge, like the Ghostbusters badge, with a red line drawn across this type of figure."

"Then otakus are outsiders," I asked, "different, but united by their outsider status?"

I don't know how good Yuka's English was, but she was correcting me before I finished my sentence.

"More like a hobbyist," Paul translated. "If it were England, you might think of trainspotters in anoraks. But then again, that's a stereotypical otaku. It's like expecting everyone in Texas to be a cowboy. There are some people like that, but most otakus are not."

Of course, I could not doubt him. I knew nothing. I was someone a Japanese would normally avoid sitting next to in the subway, leaving an empty seat in rush hour, someone who did not yet understand that it was rude to blow his big long nose in public.

But I did remember views of otakus I had not shared with my son, unsettling portraits I had found in the shadowy alleys of the World Wide Web. Most of these renderings were sexually explicit and unpleasant, but one of them, slightly less pornographic, showed an otaku, wired, connected to a woman with a keyboard in her navel. In New York I had printed out these images and filed them away in the back of a drawer.

How much clearer everything had been at home. Charley and I could sit on the Brooklyn-bound subway happily developing hypotheses about manga and Japanese history. We could be excited to realise, for instance, that manga's biggest growth occurred in the immediate postwar years when there was no television in Japan, and perhaps had taken off for just that reason. Also, in a crowded country, manga could provide a private entertainment in a public space, much as a Walkman does today. I put this theory to Yuka. But if I had expected any agreement, I was to be severely disappointed.

"Yuka can understand," Paul explained, "why you would think this."

Yuka spoke, smiling slightly.

"It is because," Paul translated, "Americans love TV so much."

Of course, I am not American and my relationship with television is far from loving, but that was beside the point. Yuka explained that manga and anime were rooted in *kamishibai,* or "paper theatre," an earlier tradition of visual storytelling. Kamishabai was particularly Japanese. It had no relation whatsoever to the West. The kamishibai man, Charley and I now learned, would travel around the city on his bicycle, on the back of which he carried pictures mounted on cards. When he arrived at a suitable park or street corner, he would bang wooden blocks together to attract an audience. Then, as the children gathered, he would set up his cards and, with these pictures and his own artful narration, beguile his audience with ghost stories, fairy stories, samurai stories, structuring them like soap operas in that every episode ended with a cliffhanger. A good kamishibai man always left his audience hungry for his next visit.

It was easy enough to understand that kamishibai might have inspired manga and that it could even be seen as a sort of movie storyboard but, this being Japan, the kamishibai business was not what it seemed. Just as the real purpose of Gundam is to sell toy robots, the real point of kamishibai was to sell sweets. The performer was primarily a candy vendor who used his stories to attract customers.

Kamishibai was still common in Japan after the war, but with increasing affluence, along with the introduction of magazines for children, its appeal diminished and a number of these candy salesmen became manga artists. What's more, famous kamishibai characters like Golden Bat became manga characters. And, as you'll see, manga characters often morphed into anime characters. Kamishibai, Yuka concluded, were essentially films on paper.

Yuka, having judged this page of history complete, then spoke animatedly for a minute or two.

"Yuka wants to say," Paul translated at last, "that the manga you see on the newsstands today grew out of the children's magazines which first appeared in the 1950s—these were monthly at first, then weekly with pictures, stories, and the graphic stories which would soon occupy whole magazines of their own—manga. By the 1960s, there was a particular sort of manga called *gekiga*, a word which just means 'action' or 'action pictures.' She is saying—this is very important—that these were aimed at kids as old as eighteen. Tokyo University students became obsessed with them, and in turn, these manga were soon reflecting their concerns about politics and, yes, sex, and sometimes violence. These students have gone on to be very successful and respectable. They are now in their fifties or sixties, but they're still reading manga. In America this does not happen. She is saying, I think, that these adult manga came, not from a lack of television, but from something more uniquely Japanese."

I asked Yuka about the transformation of manga into anime and, as Paul took notes, which he referred to as he translated, she began her answer and I understood how she might have written her seven-pound book: "When anime first appeared, it grew naturally from these paper films, because that's how manga really works, much faster than an English-language comic. Watch how quickly the people read manga on the Tokyo subway, almost like a flip book.

"The most popular manga will be made into TV animations, and the successful TV animations will in turn spawn toys, robots in particular. Astro Boy is, of course, a robot. However, the first really successful robot was Mazinga. Here, a young boy operates a robot. He goes onto the robot's head and rides it. It was Mazinga that began this robot boom in Japanese anime and it was the oil shock which ensured its continuance."

"Oil shock?" I asked.

"The oil crisis. After that, it was too expensive to have robots in live-action films. There was no question that people wanted robots, that's only natural. But because of the oil shock, the robots were all animated."

"But why this obsession with robots?"

"As I said, toys."

"Yes," I said, "and could we please explore with Yuka the feelings I had in New York watching Mobile Suit Gundam? Has she seen my questions about children at war, isolated within the belly of the beast, alienated from each other?"

Paul spoke to Yuka, who, as usual, smiled and shook her head. Charley nudged me under the table.

"Yuka says it is not like that at all. She thinks that being a pilot in a Mobile Suit is exactly like being inside a womb."

Not unsurprisingly, this was not how I'd seen these giant mechanical titan samurai as they clashed violently in the sky. "In the womb?"

Paul interpreted: "When you see these robots being knocked about and hurt, you'll notice the person operating the robot is also in pain. She says that if you think about that logically, it shouldn't happen. They should be like the guys in a military tank, getting knocked around a little roughly perhaps, but you must understand that these pilots are in the womb. They feel what the mother feels. A manga critic once said that when a person is in the womb of the robot, the robot's armour becomes that person's body. This is quite the opposite of your idea that being inside the Mobile Suit is like isolating yourself from the world. For her, it is a safe place in which you can *interact* with the world."

Later Yuka would show Charley a series of delicate drawings for some robot toys that she was hoping to have manufactured. In these sketches her feelings were made eerily clear: the robots, like pregnant women, the pilot positioned within a rotund stomach.

She wanted to know if Charley liked them.

"Yes," I translated, watching that very slight movement in the corner of his mouth. "I believe he likes them very much."

Paul then relayed this to Yuka and we waited while Yuka then spoke at length to Paul: "She says," he told us at last, "there's a Japanese word, *gutai*, for when two or more things are joined together in some way to become one. The thing about the Gundam Mobile Suits is that it's not like the tanks, it's a form of unification."

By now Tunisia had been defeated 2−0 and the corridors of Kodansha were serene once more. Our interview was almost over, but I still had not asked Yuka about her own transformation and, indeed, was shy to do so. Within one's own language or culture it might not be so difficult, but having been wrong about everything else, I was reluctant to raise this subject directly and so asked her what it meant to be not a transsexual but a visualist.

"Are there masquerades in the United States?" she asked, a little archly, I thought.

"It's like the Teddy Boys," Paul offered quickly, "or Mods or Rockers."

Perhaps it was getting late or perhaps they were just sick and tired of me, but I persisted, asking about the fastidious attention to detail, the perfectionism which seems so distinctively Japanese. But of course Yuka was the wrong person to ask. She lived inside, not outside, Japan, and it seemed she misunderstood my question.

"It would be dull if everyone was the same, wouldn't it?" she said. "Europeans are brought up thinking that if they take their clothes off they'll all turn into werewolves. Do you understand?"

"Yes," I lied. "Thank you."

8.

Transformations being something of a manga spe-
cialty, I doubt Charley would have worried about
becoming a werewolf, but he had his own reasons for
not wanting to take his clothes off in a communal
bath. At the inn, there were different bathing hours

for men and women, this being indicated by either male or female Kabuki masks hung beside the bathroom door.

"You go, Dad. That's the man's face."

"Come on. We should both do it."

"Forget it. No. No way."

If there is a finger to be pointed here, I guess it is at his parents. Although I had attended a boarding school where naked bathing was compulsory, and had lived with hippies who would have judged it "uptight" to wear a swimsuit, in New York our family maintained a more puritan aesthetic. This may have originated at the moment when Charley's older brother enquired, in a very sympathetic tone, "What happened to your penis, Mom—got old and fall off?" In any case, we were not one of those families that walked around naked, and now Charley was not about to take his pants off in front of anyone, least of all his father.

"You go," he said. "I'm going to build that Gundam model."

Well, I really should have. I had certainly bathed communally on earlier visits to Japan and enjoyed it, but now, many Toblerones and cognacs later, exhibiting the vanity of the overweight, I also chose to bathe en suite in a deep Japanese tub made not of wood but of stainless steel. Charley was perfectly happy with this bath and in ten days would use it at least three times while I, of course, suffered private guilt over my incomplete experience of the Real Japan.

My son had made his position on bathing explicit before he left New York but on the question of cuisine I had been less flexible. "We are going to eat weird things," I had told him. "We will be with Japanese people, and we are going to eat whatever we are offered, no matter how strange it looks. Okay?"

And he trained for it. At Mr. Sushi on Houston Street, he abandoned his normal California roll in favour of tuna, salmon, and octopus sashimi. I also prepared myself, acquiring a taste for the fragile slimy sea urchins that had once repulsed me.

In New York, Charley's breakfast of choice is pancakes with maple syrup. In Tokyo he began each day sitting cross-legged before a spread of fish, miso soup, seaweed, pickles, and other exotica I now forget or could never have named. At our first breakfast he was a total ace. There was nothing he would not eat.

He was just as adept at lunch and dinner with publishers and agents, and soon he was crossing the road to Fujio Takahashi's sushi bar, where our beaming host spoiled him rotten with little tidbits of God knows what while I pushed myself to my gastronomic limit, spooning up the sea urchin that tasted, of course, nothing like the *uni* at Mr. Sushi, more like—as my son informed me—live brain soup. We spurned the McDonald's down on Drunk Street, and I was proud of how my adventurous son devoured everything Mr. Takahashi placed in front of him. Paternal pride, regrettably, brings with it a certain blindness, and I was slow to notice that Charley was eating just a little less each morning. The sour pickled plums were the first to be jettisoned—so what, who cares?—next day the radish was untouched, then that white clammy stuff that doesn't taste of anything. The cold cooked fish then lost its appeal completely, and finally, on the fifth morning, Charley ate a few grains of rice and pushed aside the miso soup.

"This," he said, "is the breakfast from hell."

Fair enough. He had given it his best. I asked him what he'd rather have.

"Doughnuts," he said, "with sprinkles."

"There are no doughnuts in Japan," I said. "It is not Japanese food. Besides, we didn't come all this way to eat doughnuts."

But he was already thumb-dancing on the cell phone. "For your information," he announced, his eyes glued to the tiny screen, "Japanese people eat seven sorts of doughnuts, including American doughnuts. The Japanese word for doughnut is *donatsu*, and there is a Mister Donut across the road from the Asakusa Station."

"Okay, we can go to Mister Donut."

"Starbucks is better."

"Who was that teacher, the one who voted for Ralph Nader? Didn't he teach you that Starbucks was evil?"

"This is Japanese Starbucks."

"So?"

He grinned. "We have to experience life."

Arriving at Starbucks fifteen minutes later, we found Takashi already ensconced in a tall plush red chair that made him—uniformed as he was, and coiffed with such spiked precision—look like a member of the Earth Federation Mobile Suit carrier, White Base.

"You like muffin?" he enquired. *"Miruku?"*

The *u* ending suggested an English word recently adopted by the Japanese, but in the case of milk, that made no sense at all, so I asked Takashi was there no other word for milk.

"Oh yes, of course."

"So why do you call it miruku?"

"Miruku is more modern."

"But what's the matter with the other word?"

"Not so hygienic."

"How is that?"

"The other word is *gyuunyuu*." He wrinkled his nose. "It means liquid from udder. Miruku is better."

After days of raw fish and noodles there was something rather comforting about miruku, muffin, café latte, and we spread ourselves out, the boys with cell phones and Game Boys and three-inch-thick mangas which you buy at railway stations for a quarter. Charley had also brought an autographed Gundam book as a gift for Takashi, who examined Tomino's signature very closely before turning to me.

"Carey-san, where do you wish to go? Perhaps I can help you?"

When I'd planned the coming evening I had had no idea that Takashi existed, and now I would have given almost anything to include him. "Tonight," I said, "we have an appointment in Minato-ku."

"Perhaps there are more interesting places I could take you?"

"Thank you, Takashi, but a friend of mine lives there. We are going to watch *My Neighbor Totoro* in his apartment." If I thought that mentioning this famous anime would placate him, I was wrong.

"Oh yes, *Totoro* is nice. Children like it very much," he said, and I suspected that he now wished to share his animus against *Totoro* with Charley. "You have not seen it in New York? When you were younger, Charley?"

"A few times."

"So why come to Japan to watch what you have already seen?"

"It's for my dad's book."

"We want to understand it in a Japanese way," I said, "so we are watching it with a Japanese friend."

Takashi considered this, his head cocked thoughtfully to one side. "Yes," he said, "foreigners cannot understand us, but if you wish, you could come to my grandmother's apartment."

I understood, even at the moment, that he was honouring us by inviting us into his home. I thought also that his grandmother might be thrown into total disarray at having to entertain two gaijin. Just the same, it was with real regret that we declined the invitation.

"If you like," said Takashi, "you can come to my grandmother's apartment and I will show you tapes of Mobile Suit Gundam never released in America. I will translate. Perhaps you like Miyazaki, but he is the Japanese Walt Disney. You have your own Walt Disney." He widened his large eyes, which at that moment seemed as if they'd been drawn by Uncle Walt himself.

Hayao Miyazaki has often been compared to

Walt Disney, but neither this nor the fact that Disney owns American rights to most of Miyazaki's work makes this comparison remotely apt. Miyazaki is a great, not merely successful, artist and *My Neighbor Totoro* a truly masterful film that can sustain frequent viewings, a far more serious accomplishment than, say, *Bambi* or *Snow White*.

"But tomorrow," I said, "we are going to Mr. Miyazaki's Ghibli Museum with some other Japanese friends. Perhaps we could get tickets for you. We are hoping we might meet Mr. Miyazaki there."

"You will never meet Mr. Miyazaki," Takashi said sternly. "I am very sorry, but whoever has promised this is wrong. All Japanese people know this. I myself prefer the work of Mr. Tomino, who as you probably know worked with Osamu Tezuka on *Astro Boy* and you have already met with him. But Mr. Miyazaki is more difficult to meet than Walt Disney."

"Takashi," I said, "Walt Disney is dead."

"His point," said Charley.

"I will draw you a map," said Takashi. "How to come to my grandmother's. And from his jacket pocket he produced a piece of fine onionskin paper on which he then drew the most exquisite map. "For my grandmother, you should bring a small gift. I will show you where to have it wrapped."

"But Takashi, we already have an appointment tonight."

"Just the same," said the wilful young man, "perhaps the other appointment can be changed."

Charley has this map still, amongst his collected treasures of Japan. It is very beautiful indeed, but every time I look at it I remember Takashi's upset face as he left Starbucks that day.

"I think he's hurt, Dad."

"What could I do?"

"I know."

"We have to see Kenji."

"I know."

Across the street, the first tourists of the day were entering the arcade of food, kitsch, commercial opportunism, which would lead them to the very beautiful reconstructed temple of Sensoji. Soon, on the way to visit the temple, we would buy a tiny plastic statue of a Mobile Suit, but for now we stayed in Starbucks, guilty and miserable.

9.

"All I want," I had said to Kenji, "is to watch a video with you." What I had in mind was to freeze Miyazaki's images at will and ask him questions about anything I didn't understand.

Kenji is a busy architect with a Tokyo practice,

and I really had no right to make such a request. Kenji was gracious and too generous to even hint as much, not for a second, but the questions of *where* and *how* to watch this video were not easily answered. Our ryokan would have no VCR, so that was out. Kenji was living at that time with his parents. To see the video there, I assumed, would have raised more problems than a foreigner could begin to imagine.

AGGHHHH, as they say in manga.

"Perhaps," Kenji said, "we could watch it in my office," but I could see he was worried about this too, possibly because this venue might appear less hospitable than he would like.

In the end, however, this is exactly where we found ourselves, although "office" hardly describes a space so conspicuously empty of anything that would identify itself as such. I don't mean to suggest that it was minimalist, only that it was unusually large and there was nothing much in it. Was there a mystery here? I seriously doubt it, although this is how it is with travelling—the simplest things take on an air of great inscrutability and so many questions arise, only to be half born and then lost as they are bumped aside by others. The most mundane events take on the character of deep secrets.

I remember being seated next to a pugnacious

New York celebrity at dinner. When I asked him a question, he glowered at me and said, "Are you interviewing me?"

"You better hope not," I told him. "I'm a terrible reporter."

I have not one note on the location of Kenji's office. I have a vague memory of expensive-looking apartment houses and a paucity of shops. Inside, floating on a beige or off-white carpet was a sofa, a chair, a VCR and monitor.

I expected Charley to be pining for his friend Takashi, but Kenji had provided the most interesting tourist experience of all: exotic junk food in plastic bags. There were three different sorts of junk food but when, months later, I asked Charley what he had eaten, only one item had stuck in his mind. "It was like a cylinder," he said, "and it was sort of crunchy, and there was, whatchamacallit, fine brown sugar so it was really sweet. It tasted sort of weird, but it was very good."

Thus set up, with a very large bottle of Coca-Cola between us, we began to watch one of the masterpieces of Japanese animation.

Totoro finally resolves itself as a charming hymn to animism, a world of ghosts and spirits, in particular the spirit of the forest. It does this by telling the story of two young girls who, with their father, move to an old-fashioned house in the country while their mother is in hospital. Like all of Miyazaki's work, the film exhibits the most pleasurably detailed physical world, landscape in all its complexity, and architecture so keenly observed that one immediately recognises it was drawn from life. This is something far richer and more sophisticated than the flat, cute world of Disney.

Miyazaki's production company is Ghibli (from which *Grave of the Fireflies* also emerged) and in the Ghibli Museum you can flip through huge volumes of location photographs and see the director's sketches pinned to the wall and lying loosely on the tables, as casually as in an artist's untidy office. Part of Miyazaki's magic is the way he introduces his cartoon characters—exaggerated in a way that the landscapes and architecture are not—into this keenly examined real world. This is not to suggest that the depictions of the human figures are less truthful or detailed. Indeed, one of the film's great pleasures is the very compelling characterisation, and the joy this can stir in the viewer's heart.

The film begins with father and daughters travelling in a small van, their possessions strapped down onto its roof. The girls are full of wonder. They pass a capped man riding a bicycle across a bridge. "Mei!" calls the ten-year-old to her four-year-old sister. "Hide, Mei." Then, a moment later, she says, "It's okay, it's not a policeman."

So what does this mean? But the film moves so fast that I didn't ask Kenji to pause the tape until a moment later, to wonder what their voices revealed about the characters.

"That they are city people," he said. "That they use a sort of polite pronunciation, and that the father, when he talks to them, is well educated."

The road passes through fields, over a bridge, turns a corner and now we see how rural this is, nothing like the concreted landscape Alex Kerr attacks so eloquently in *Lost Japan*. The road is unsealed, rutted.

"Stop," said Kenji.

As Charley and I had already seen the film three times, the image Kenji froze was so familiar that it was hard to imagine what else we might learn from it. The right-hand side of the frame was dominated by the trunks of two huge trees; the gloom of the woods was deep, and one already felt the force of nature. What Kenji now pointed out, what Charley and I had never noticed, was that hidden in the shadows were some steps and a *torii*, a red gate to a shrine, an early hint of the film's religious reverence for nature. This is so subtle, though, that we're more likely to notice that the truck is a three-wheeler, that it splashes through a puddle beside the two big trees, and emerges into a bright landscape of rice paddies. It is part of Miyazaki's genius that as he celebrates the world of nature, trees, flowers, as the girls look into a stream and exclaim about a fish, he also shows us an empty sake bottle abandoned in the water, and that this is done in some morally neutral way.

"You can see," Kenji said, "that this is set twenty or thirty years ago."

In fact, this had not occurred to me.

"Perhaps," he said, "it is Miyazaki's childhood. What tells us that this is so long ago? Well, firstly the three-wheeled van, and then the local bus it passes. See the model. He is not being romantic about the countryside but he is perhaps nostalgic about his childhood, and for a physical world that, while not pristine then, has been seriously messed-up since."

The three characters finally arrive at the house on foot. To my eye, it is a simple farmhouse, run-down, rustic, but also particularly Japanese. The first time I saw the film, I wished to live in that house, and it was because of this that I thought it might be interesting to watch it with an architect, to extract all the information that was before my eyes but culturally inaccessible. Now Kenji explained that this was in fact two houses, an old house with a modern addition, a Western-style front constructed in perhaps the 1920s.

Western? It had seemed so Japanese.

Wonderfully, this was not the only misunderstanding. First, Kenji told us, this dusty, slightly run-down house belonged to a rich family. "Who else could afford such a luxury? Also," he said, "it is a kind of a ghost house."

"What makes it a ghost house?"

"Well, as you will see in a moment, there is a well."

"So?"

"The well is a very animistic thing. It is a hole to another world, to ghosts and spirits. A Japanese viewer sees that well and immediately understands that this will be a story about spirits. Besides—there!—the older girl is calling. She says, This is like a haunted house."

A moment later we see how this notion is developed: girls play, running, whooping, performing handsprings which serve to draw them (and us) from the house and into nature. Suddenly we are confronted by a vast and ancient camphor tree which looms like a mountain above the children. This tree will be a major character in the story, the world of the wonderful mythic Totoro. But only after the girls enter the house, and a single nut drops mysteriously to the floor, do we really begin to feel the place is haunted.

It is just at this point, as the father offers rational explanations—squirrels, perhaps, or acorn mice—that Miyazaki shows us that well, which in New York City had seemed merely commonplace, utilitarian.

Then the girls open the back door. It is bright outside, dark inside. As the door swings open, we see tiny black creatures and hear a high-pitched sort of "squittering" as they flee the light. We are reminded of both bats and cockroaches, but these are neither.

The girls scream but then, without reference to each other, square their shoulders and march forward, an action that not only strengthens the drama, but also commences an architectural tour. By freezing the frame at any point, we could have had a tutorial on the Japanese house, but let us move forward to the bathroom. "Father, Father," the girls call. "There's something in here."

"What?"

"We don't know. Squirrels? Not cockroaches. Not mice."

The father peers inside the bath and there, rendered in loving detail, is a Japanese soaking tub (the history of which might be a book in itself), where later we will see the family bathe together. Kenji will point out that the bathroom is illuminated solely by light "stolen" from the kitchen next door, which is not only architecturally ingenious, but perfectly revealing of how Japanese families traditionally bathed, with no shred of shame or immodesty.

Meanwhile, the girls are still excited about these spooky little black things they have seen.

"Ah so," says the father (yes, really, that is what he says). "It must be makkuro kurosuke."

"Makkuro kurosuke?"

"The black spots that appear in front of your eyes," he explains, "when you come inside on a bright day."

The girls laugh. "Come on out, makkuro kurosuke. Come out or we'll pull your eyes out."

Miyazaki then undercuts this rational explanation, showing us these black dust bunnies scuttling into a drainpipe by the children's feet.

"Okay," the father says, "now we need to find the stairs to the second floor. Can you do this for me? We need to open the windows." The children run off and our architectural tour continues, as fine a tour as you could find in any museum. This is at once a real house and a vividly imagined one, filled everywhere with particular detail: shoji with two transparent panels in each; a circular window between rooms; tatami over which the children, shoes still on their feet, must walk on their knees.

Very soon there will be more drama, nuts falling and strange little black spirits rustling, skittering from the light. Mei catches one and carries it downstairs, trapped like a mosquito in her hands, and from here the story moves relentlessly forward to her meeting with the Totoro, the spirit of the woods, and introduces us to the sick mother, who unlike the stock figure in an American movie neither dies nor returns home.

That night in Minato-ku, Charley fell asleep quite early. He had, after all, seen the film many times already and the purpose of this particular viewing was not to annotate it to death but to understand that this beautiful entertainment contained a whole history and culture hidden between the frames.

We then arrived, however, at the most exciting example of hidden signs. High in the ceiling of the attic, where Mei caught the dust bunny, there is an ornament, no more commented on than the red gate to the shrine or the simple rope around the camphor tree indicating that it's sacred. Though the director does nothing to draw our attention to it, I recall the paper decoration hanging from the ridgepole looked something like a bird. It would have existed, Kenji explained, from the time construction on the house began. We were now talking not of figments made of pixels but of actual substances. During construction the ornament on the ridgepole would have been blown by the wind and drenched by rain until it was torn and tattered. Once there was a roof to shelter it, this weathered talisman would have been tucked down into the attic and kept there, protected, for good luck. All this Charley would learn in the morning; for now, at his father's favourite part, he was emitting a sweet adenoidal snore.

Kenji found Charley a quilt and went on to tell me that Japanese carpenters are often—unlike their visualist cousins in Shinjuku—very religious. A great many Shinto ceremonies are associated with the construction of a house and these are part of Kenji's life in Tokyo today. He began describing ceremonies with rice and salt and sake and I later found the same information in William Coaldrake's *Way of the Carpenter,* which is far more quotable than my so-called reporter's notebook: "Young bamboo stalks are used to mark the four corners of a sacred enclosure on the building site," he writes. "These are joined by a sacred rope of new straw (hymenia) bearing sacred, folded white invocatory papers. An altar is erected with a separate table for offerings of rice, salt, fruit and sake.... The most important ceremony, celebrating completion of the assembly of the timber frame, is the ridge-raising ceremony (*joutoushiki* or *muneageshiki*). It includes the ceremonial raising and positioning of the ridgepole, thanksgiving for the safe erection of the frame, and prayers for the long life and well-being of the building and its inhabitants.... In traditional practice, the chief master carpenter himself frequently officiated at the ceremonies, donning the robes of a Shinto priest.... The chief master carpenter was formerly responsible for making the ritual implements and decorations for these ceremonies, such as the ridge plaque and sacred bow and arrow that were attached to the ridgepole during the ridge-raising ceremony, but this practice has largely lapsed."

Sometime around ten we rewound the tape, still only one-third played, and Kenji, kind as ever, drove us back to Asakusa, where we slipped through the narrow lanes moving bicycles aside as if playing a life-sized game of checkers that would finally lead us to our tatami-matted room where all seven pounds of *Gundam Officials, Limited Edition* was placed reverently in the tokonoma.

"I feel sorry for Takashi," said Charley. "I think he might be mad at me."

"Why? For visiting Kenji instead of his grandmother?"

"No, because I'm going to see Mr. Miyazaki.

Maybe he thinks I am not loyal to Mr. Tomino."

"No," I said. "I'm sure that's not true. Did you clean your teeth?"

"Yes," he lied, and immediately fell into a sleep from which he would not be woken.

10.

We would have been wiser to have breakfasted on fish and miso. There was a long, long day ahead, an interview with the elusive Mr. Kitakubo of *Blood: The Last Vampire* and then a tour of the Ghibli Museum and a visit to Miyazaki's studio. Our schedule had protein written all over it, but we were weary of live fish and dead fish and battered fish and fish with skewers stuck up their little bottoms. So we left the ryokan, and headed in search of Mister Donut, stepping wide of the early-morning alcoholics feeding their hundred-yen coins into the sake machine on the corner, past the kids with their black hair stripped back to a dangerous-looking anime brown, then crossing over the bridge at the Asakusa View Hotel to the other side of Kokusai Street, where weaving bicyclists sliced between us, quiet and polite as death itself. At last, thank God, we finally located Mister Donut, where we discovered, to our huge surprise, none other than he who had so subtly steered Charley to Starbucks.

There stood Takashi, no longer a Mobile Suit pilot, but a teenage employee, dressed neatly in a multicoloured uniform with *Mister Donut*™ embroidered on its pocket. In this role he would not acknowledge us, unless you interpreted the rising glow in his cheeks as a form of recognition. Takashi was in character, completely. He was Mister Donut himself. He greeted us as customers, as strangers to be respected and served, issuing that singsong welcome that Paul told me had its origins in the Yoshiwara Pleasure Gardens, whose courtesans developed a kind of lingua franca understood by all the powerful visitors from distant provinces, a polite greeting that echoes centuries later at the entrance to every department store in Tokyo.

"*Trasshaimase,*" he said, in unison with his workmates. "Please?" he enquired, his expression sugar-glazed, no sprinkles.

"Two doughnuts," I said. "One milk, one coffee."

"Stay or go?" he enquired, his English as American as his menu.

"To stay," I said, then regretted it, for I had just glimpsed the fury in his eyes.

Moments later we were carrying our trays to the farthermost corner where Charley would neither eat nor look at me.

"Come on. This is not my fault."

"I *told* you," he whispered. "Takashi thinks we are disloyal to Mr. Tomino."

"That's ridiculous."

"Not to him, Dad. He can't understand how we can go to Studio Ghibli either."

"More likely he doesn't want us to see him here. He can't be proud of working here. It's like Mc-Donald's."

We ate our doughnuts in sugary misery, and when we left for our meeting with the director of *Blood: The Last Vampire*, we shared no more intimacy with our former friend than that offered by the Yoshiwara farewell—although I did notice that Takashi's bow was very low indeed, and I suspected him of sarcasm such as I had suffered, many years before, in the house of a Japanese friend's father who had fought Australians and despised us all.

It was not until we were on the train that Charley spoke. "I still have his cell phone," he said.

"Good, we can text-message him."

"No. But I have to give it back."

"We'll take it to him tomorrow. In the morning, before we leave."

"We should buy him a gift, Dad. He was really nice to us."

"Yes, very kind."

"We should have taken him to meet Mr. Tomino. That would have made him really happy."

"Well, I think he was too shy, but I should have offered anyway."

"Yes," said Charley. "And it would have been easy to take him to dinner with the otaku, to that place, you know, with that guy." He was referring to the evening we'd spent in a Shinjuku restaurant patronised by manga artists, where the producer of the hugely popular anime and manga series One Piece taught him tricks requiring not a word of English, and where Yuka the otaku leaned behind my back and whispered to Charley, "Shush, big secret, there is a new Mobile Suit Gundam series, very soon." And the mama-san had once been a famous radio announcer, and the master of the house was from a samurai family and now, suffering from emphysema, was sucking oxygen through plastic tubes, sitting grandly, cross-legged, while taking our orders. Gathered all around us were manga writers, artists, anime producers, publishers like Irie-san from Kodansha. Here someone had produced the latest *Shonen Jump*, a best-selling manga, warm off the presses, in which a huge spread depicted our host himself, a samurai with plastic tubes and a bevy of cute cartoon nurses tending him. We were, at that giddy moment, at the red-hot centre of the manga world, or so it felt to both of us.

"We definitely should have brought along Takashi," he said.

"Charley, we never knew where we were going. We were halfway through dinner before we really understood where we were."

"We could have called him," Charley said.

"Yes, we should have."

But still, of course, we were without him, on our way to meet the most difficult of all our subjects, or the one most difficult to arrange an appointment with. We waited with Jerry and Etsuko in that cheesy coffee shop Jerry had so carefully chosen, the sort of place where you order fries and cappuccino; and this, as far as I remember, is what we did until the famous director of *Blood: The Last Vampire* showed up.

Given the negotiations with his production company, Mr. Kitakubo was not at all what I had expected, and at the same time he was much more like a cartoon artist than anyone we'd met so far. He was in his twenties, fairly short, with black hair, a skimpy thin moustache and a slightly shy, roguish way of smiling. I liked him immediately. He looked like an underprivileged kid who had grown up drawing manga by the light of the open refrigerator door. Of course, I might be hopelessly wrong, but he seemed more "street," less groomed than the strangely encoded, visually fastidious work he had directed.

To Etsuko he bowed, with me he shook hands, but on being introduced to Charley he gave that complex shoulder-slamming handshake, and they performed the complete set of moves without a moment of misunderstanding. But if that suggests he'd been somehow fatally Americanised, let me tell you, Fremantle Jack, it was not that simple. In fact, Mr. Kitakubo responded to my written questions in the same style as every other damn Japanese I'd questioned. That is, he made it clear that nothing in this country was as I thought it was. My misunderstandings were very interesting, he said. By which he did not mean to claim that his film did not have meanings—of course it did—but after a long, exhausting Q&A it became clear that he would reveal none of them to me.

All this was offered in the most polite and humble manner, but I was losing the will to conduct this sort of interrogation. I was delighted to have liked his film. I was happy to have my own ideas about it, but I knew it was impossible to winkle from him his feelings about foreigners, America, the Vietnam War, swords, decapitation, evisceration, soldiers, aliens, Commodore Perry, and Douglas MacArthur. Really, the best thing that happened in that coffee shop was to see my son get all he had wanted in the first place: a photo op with the director of *Blood: The Last Vampire.* For this, and this only, he had endured hours of boring talk.

After we bid good-bye to Mr. Kitakubo, I really had little interest in visiting the Ghibli Museum. As Takashi had said, we would not meet Mr. Miyazaki, but by now that was almost a relief. I was weary of pulling out my lists of questions, of having insights that were apparently only figments of my foreign imagination, of forgetting to bring my business cards along to meetings conducted with all the formality of the Treaty of Versailles. I happily would have cancelled the afternoon's excursion had not Mrs. Yoko Miyagi, who translates my novels into Japanese, pursued Studio Ghibli on my behalf.

It was impossible to get tickets on such short notice. Everyone said so. Even if you were Japanese. Even if you lived in Tokyo. It was harder, said Kenji, than getting midcourt seats at a Knicks game in Madison Square Garden.

I'm not sure if Mrs. Miyagi had known of the level of difficulty this presented or even if she knew who Hayao Miyazaki was, but she got us tickets to the museum and she made sure we could be admitted to the studio itself. Because Miyazaki had just finished *The Cat's Return*, there would probably be nothing to look at except blank monitors and empty chairs, but it seemed a miracle that she got us in the door. Also, I understood that she made a valiant attempt to persuade the organisation that Mr. Miyazaki should meet with us, though this, it appeared, was totally impossible. He was very famous, very busy, and he was about to go to Europe.

Yoko Miyagi is a wonderful woman, small as a sparrow, but so endowed with energy and intelligence as to constitute a force of nature. It was not difficult to imagine her pushing at the walls of Studio Ghibli until they yielded.

At the studio we were met by an executive whose name—so many cards—I could not recall when I got home, but it was very, very clear to me that our presence was a puzzle, possibly even an annoyance. Did I have a card? What did I want to know? The film was made, the party over. There was nothing to show but an empty production facility.

"Fantastic," I said, surveying nothing much.

What did I wish to ask?

We sat at a table, had a soda then the tour. We looked over the shoulders of young animators working at their computer monitors, at a woman colouring a cel. My comments were trite. "Computers! How amazing!" This, it seemed, was what the trip had come to: everything falling apart, Takashi offended, Studio Ghibli looking desolate, a looted museum in the last days of a war.

Now all of the above is what I *thought* was happening. Yet later, when I checked my version of events with Mrs. Miyagi, I learned I had been horribly mistaken.

"I must admit," she wrote, "after reading the scene in the cafeteria at Studio Ghibli I became quite worried that I gave you the wrong impression.

"After I wrote to you in New York to suggest the visit, I learned that the tickets were sold out, so I was in trouble, and phoned the museum for help. Someone there suggested I talk to the manager of publicity at the studio, Mr. Nishioka (the man we met). I explained the purpose of your visit, that it was very short, and that you were looking at aspects of Japanese culture through the lens of anime and manga.

"He knew your name and your novel *Oscar and Lucinda* and kindly offered us the opportunity to visit. I never pushed him at all. I don't like to push anyone! Mr. Nishioka informed me that Mr. Miyazaki was going abroad shortly and that meeting him would be unlikely, but still he allowed us to visit."

Thus, as we passed from one empty office to another, I saw it through the lens of a foreigner's misunderstanding. I made notes which I would later, fortunately, be unable to read, although I do vividly remember the moment when the man I now know as Mr. Nishioka said, "This is where Mr. Miyazaki works."

And there, across the counter, I saw a compact man with a grey beard. It was Hayao Miyazaki, walking toward Charley and extending his hand. Perhaps I bowed.

"Of course," Yoko wrote, "I was as surprised as

anyone when Mr. Miyazaki appeared and introduced himself. He seemed to really enjoy explaining his work to you and Charley, and I was thrilled that you could get to meet him."

Mr. Miyazaki opened a drawer and took out a little book, which he showed my son. He flipped the pages and figures danced across the top corners as in a silent film.

Mr. Nishioka was now smiling, which surprised me. Mr. Miyazaki looked around for other things that might entertain us. He opened another drawer. He had little English. We had no Japanese. He flipped a second book, and we all laughed. By now the most famous anime director in the world was doing show-and-tell. He was the kamishibai man dashing his wooden blocks together and working the magic of paper film.

He took us to the computer and showed a new work that featured the grandmother of the magical animated cat-bus that Totoro had ridden on. And, thank God, we had no language. Thank God, there were no questions to ask, just the privilege of sharing the joy of a great artist telling a story to an audience.

He took us over to his pinboard, and I saw he'd been collecting works of nineteenth-century science fiction, the graphic equivalents of Jules Verne. Had I spoken Japanese, I might have confessed to having a similar fascination but what would be the point of that?

Mr. Miyazaki pushed his English to the limit. I nodded and made notes but what I was thinking was, "There is Charley standing next to Hayao Miyazaki and I have left my damn camera in the hotel."

Then, somehow, there was Mrs. Miyagi with her camera, and there was Charley standing next to God. I never wondered how that might have happened, but when the flash went off I knew my son had the biggest prize of all.

"When I went downstairs to get my camera," Mrs. Miyagi wrote later, "I noticed on the way back that I had forgotten to put film in it. Mr. Nishioka ran back and retrieved it for me. He was very kind."

Even then, before she had reason to have her suspicions confirmed, it must have been clear to Mrs. Miyagi that I was confused. That night when we arrived back at the ryokan, there was a fax waiting: "I'm afraid," she wrote with typical modesty, "you couldn't understand my poor English at Studio Ghibli, so I think I should clarify what Director Miyazaki said in more detail.

"He said that he thinks one of the most important of man's abilities is the imagination, so the purpose of his creative activities is to develop the imagination of children, the coming generations. Imagination can create a totally different world, depending on its use. It can give birth to virtue, or destructive weapons which threaten the whole world. He mentioned being afraid of the potential risk."

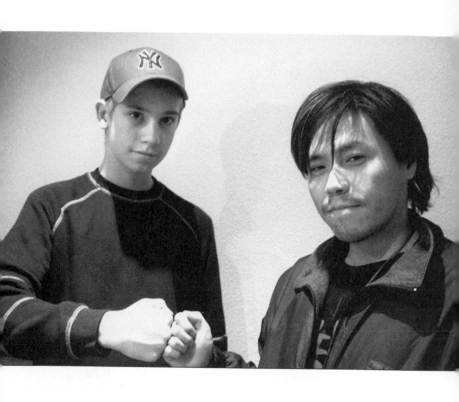

11.

The following morning was an awful rush. Hurriedly, we crammed all the gifts, books, assembled robots, kits, brochures of Japanese toilets, editions of Tanizaki, and rolls of film into our bags. We also had our weighty *Gundam Officials, Limited Edition* and now Charley wanted to go shopping for *wrapping paper*.

"Why? We need a new suitcase for all this junk, so what do you need wrapping paper for?"

"I am giving this"—he held up the book Yuka and Paul and Irie-san had spent so much time and money producing for Kodansha—"to Takashi."

I am a good enough traveller until the day I have to catch the plane, but then I become an anxious fool, following a schedule which inevitably lands me at the airport five hours early. I hate the way I do this, but as usual I turned everything into a panic. I bought a case. I found wrapping paper. Finally we came down the stairs of the hotel in a great mess of bags and parcels, paid the bill, somehow communicated to the taxi driver that we wished to stop at Mister Donut en route to Tokyo Station. So far, so good. We came down Kokusai Street and there it was.

But Mister Donut was closed. Impossible. We both got out of the car and stood with our noses pressed against the glass doors. It had been open before, so how could it be closed now? I took the parcel from my son and laid it on the step.

Charley retrieved his gift and then, from deep in a pocket of his baggy jeans, pulled out the map Takashi had drawn when he invited us to his grandmother's apartment.

"Oh no," I thought, "no, please, no."

But what was I to do? My only choice was to hand the driver our map. "We go," I said in perfect English.

"Okay," he said, and closed the doors.

"Very far? Long distance?"

"Okay," he said, reading the map, driving the car, swinging into a little lane.

I did not know if this was a good sign or a bad sign, that we were not heading for a freeway.

"Shitamachi?"

"Shitamachi," he agreed.

Before long we were deep in the maze of old downtown Tokyo, twisting, turning, backtracking to avoid stubborn sanitation trucks and officious policemen. But finally we arrived at a low dun-coloured building next to a very homely tempura bar.

The driver pointed.

Charley opened the car door, already juggling the heavy gift and little cell phone.

"Do you want me to come?"

"No," he said.

He knocked on the door, only twelve years old but already five feet eight and square-shouldered, filling the door of that small one-storyed house. Almost a man, I thought, but then, without warning, the taxi driver tore away, leaving my little boy behind.

"Hey!" I cried.

"Okay," said the driver. "Okay."

Then I understood. We had been blocking traffic. I was not to worry. He was going to circle. He did so very quickly, and when we returned Charley had been joined in the street by an elderly woman in a kimono. Takashi's Kabuki-loving grandmother, or so I guessed.

As the taxi pulled up opposite, Charley presented the gift—very beautifully, I thought—and then bowed to the woman.

She bowed to him and suddenly, unexpectedly, leaned forward and kissed his cheek.

And that was it. Charley climbed in, blushing just a little. The driver slammed the door shut, and we waved good-bye.

"I was surprised she kissed you," I said. "I didn't think they did that."

"Must be the Real Japan," he said.

"Yes," I said.

"Found it finally," Charley said. "Let's get out of here before we learn we're wrong."

Grateful acknowledgment is made to the following for permission to reprint
previously published and unpublished material:

Jeremy Hedley: Excerpt from facsimile correspondence between Jeremy Hedley
and Peter Carey. Reprinted by permission of Jeremy Hedley.

Jon Kessler: Excerpt from an article written with Timothy Blum. Copyright ©
by Jon Kessler and Timothy Blum. Reprinted by permission of Jon Kessler.

The New York Times Agency: Excerpt from "Tokyo Journal" by James Brooke
from *The New York Times* (April 7, 2003). Copyright © 2003 by
The New York Times Co. Reprinted by permission of The New York Times Agency.

A NOTE ON THE TYPE

The text of this book was set in Requiem, created in the 1990s by the Hoefler Type Foundry. It was derived from a set of inscriptional capitals appearing in Ludovico Vicentino degli Arrighi's 1523 writing manual, *Il Modo de Temperare le Penne*. A master scribe, Arrighi is remembered as an exemplar of the chancery italic, a style revived in Requiem Italic.

Composed by North Market Street Graphics,
Lancaster, Pennsylvania
Printed and bound by R. R. Donnelley & Sons,
Harrisonburg, Virginia
Designed by Chip Kidd

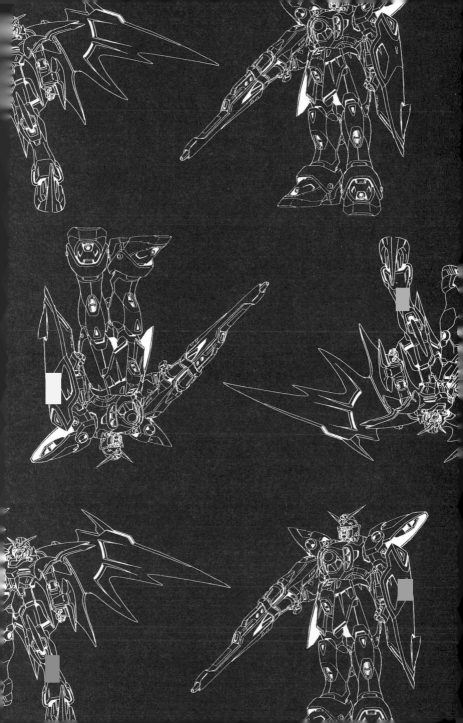

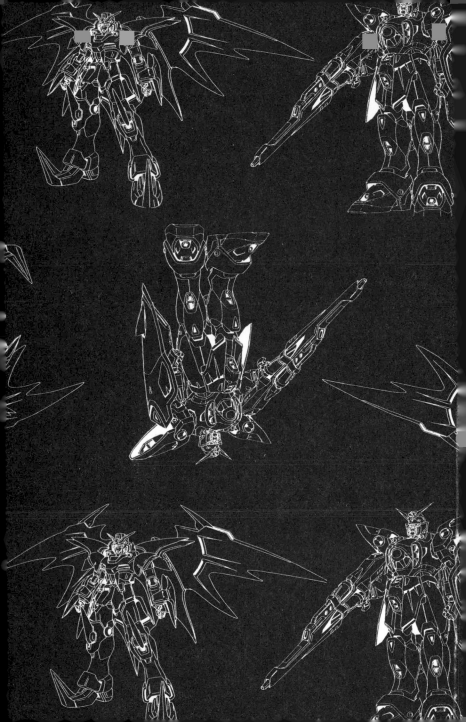